Bible Study Guide

Man's Relationship To His Eternal God

by
Rev. J. A. Jefferson

authorHOUSE®

AuthorHouse™
1663 Liberty Drive, Suite 200
Bloomington, IN 47403
www.authorhouse.com
Phone: 1-800-839-8640

First published by AuthorHouse 3/10/2009

ISBN: 978-1-4389-0411-5 (sc)

Printed in the United States of America
Bloomington, Indiana

This book is printed on acid-free paper.

Quotations are from the Authorized or the King James Version of the Bible

ABOUT THE AUTHOR

The author has studied the Bible from the time he was solemnly and publicly set apart in 1985 and ordained to the work of the gospel ministry by the authority and order of the Sixteenth Street Baptist Church under the Reverend Curtis Kyle. The author was publicly ordained in 1990 to the work of the Gospel Ministry to the views of the Holy Bible Doctrine in the Christian Faith of the Pentecostal Church.

The author received instruction in Part I and II of the Old and New Testament at Howard University in 1977. He was a member of the 1988 Ministry Class at the Jericho Christian Training Center, Washington, DC; attended Chaplain Moral Leadership Staff College at Dover College, Dover, Delaware in 1988; then completed further studies in Moral Leadership at the Middle East Region Chaplain's Staff College at Dover Air Force Base, Dover, Maryland in 2000. That same year he recieved the Chaplain of the Year Award.

After serving as chaplain for the District of Columbia Jail, author became chaplain for the District of Columbia Department of Corrections under the federal government from 1997 until 2004. The author joined the Chaplain Department at the District of Columbia General Hospital in 1985 and served diligently until his retirement in 2004. He also served as police Clergy with the Philadelphia Police Department and for 9 years volunteered as a Big Brother in the District of Columbia.

Chaplain John A. Jefferson
email:jj2558@bellsouth.net

PREFACE

THIS BIBLE STUDY GUIDE IS INTENDED TO ASSIST THOSE WHO ARE SEEKING A CLEARER UNDERSTANDING OF THE TEACHINGS OF THE BIBLE-GOD'S HOLY WRITTEN WORD. IT IS INTENDED FOR USE BY THOSE WHO WANT TO STRENGTHEN THEIR CHRISTIAN LIFE THROUGH FELLOWSHIP AND STUDY. IT WILL ACT AS A GUIDE FOR PERSONAL AND GROUP STUDY AND EXPLAIN MANY ASPECTS OF MAN'S RELATIONSHIP IN HIS ETERNAL GOD.

READING THE WORD OF GOD FOCUSES OUR THOUGHTS AND ACTIONS TO THE UNITY OF THE SPIRIT OF PEACE. "THE FRUIT OF RIGHTOUSNESS IS SOWN IN PEACE OF THEM THAT MAKE PEACE" (JAMES 3:18). ALONG WITH THIS STUDY GUIDE BELIEVERS ARE CHARGED WITH SERVING EACH OTHER WITH THE UTMOST LOVE AND RESPECT. THE BIBLE TEACHES US TO CHOOSE THIS DAY WHO WE WILL SERVE; WE ARE CALLED OUT OF DARKNESS INTO THAT WONDERFUL LIGHT (1-PETER 2:9). CHRISTIANS ARE SPECIAL PEOPLE WHO ANSWER GOD'S CALL. THEY BECOME FILLED WITH THE FRUITS OF RIGHTOUSNESS, WHICH IS BY JESUS CHRIST, UNTO THE GLORY AND PRAISE TO GOD.

SALVATION IS WROUGHT BY THE FATHER, THE SON AND THE HOLY SPIRIT. GOD THE FATHER IS THE CREATOR OF HEAVEN AND EARTH WHO SENT HIS SON TO BE THE PERFECT SACRIFICE FOR OUR SINS. WE NEED ONLY ACCEPT THE GIFT OF SALVATION PROVIDED BY OUR LOVING GOD THROUGH JESUS CHRIST. JESUS PROMISED TO RETURN ONE DAY AND WE ARE TO BE READY. READING AND STUDYING THE BIBLE WILL TEACH US HOW TO BE READY AND BE THE BEST WE CAN BE FOR THE GLORY OF GOD THROUGH JESUS CHRIST.

Reverend J. A. Jefferson

Table of Contents

UNIT V: PRAYERS

UNIT I: GOD'S FRAMEWORK OF TIME AND SPACE

Man lives within a framework of time and space created by God. God exists eternally and will remove the limits of time and space so that man can relate to God in an eternal relationship.

GOD THE CREATOR

As creator, God brought the world into being—even before the beginning of time itself. He will also bring the world to its ultimate conclusion in accordance with His will and purpose.

Gen 1:1 *In the beginning God created the heaven and the earth.*

UNITS OF TIME CREATED BY GOD

The concept of time is set forth in the Bible. We define time is a measurable period during which an action or condition exists or continues. For the Hebrew people, units of time were measured in hours, day, weeks, months, and years.

TIME IS IN GOD'S HANDS

Time is in the hands of God. Man is warned not to plan his time as if it belonged to him, but to do what the Lord wills in his life. Therefore, the time to accept salvation is now. Man is to seek and trust the Lord at all times and practice righteousness during his life here on the earth. Since the days are evil, the Christian believer is to make the most of the time that has been given him.

Eccles 9:12 *For man also knoweth not his time: as the fishes that are taken in an evil net, and as the birds that are caught in the snare; so are the sons of men snared in an evil time, when it falleth suddenly upon them.*

Psalms 31:15 *My times are in thy hand: deliver me from the hand of mine enemies, and from them that persecute me.*

1. Man is to do the will of God.

James 4:13 *Go to now, ye that say, To day or to morrow we will go into such a city, and continue there a year, and buy and sell, and get gain:*

James 4:14 *Whereas ye know not what shall be on the morrow. For what is your life? It is even a vapour, that appeareth for a little time, and then vanisheth away.*

James 4:15 *For that ye ought to say, If the Lord will, we shall live, and do this, or that.*

James 4:16 *But now ye rejoice in your boastings: all such rejoicing is evil.*

2. The day of Salvation is near.

2 Cor 6:2 *(For he saith, I have heard thee in a time accepted, and in the day of salvation have I succoured thee: behold, now is the accepted time; behold, now is the day of salvation.)*

3.   Practice righteousness and seek the Lord.

Hosea 10:12 *Sow to yourselves in righteousness, reap in mercy; break up your fallow ground: for it is time to seek the LORD, till he come and rain righteousness upon you.*

Psalms 106:3 *Blessed are they that keep judgment, and he that doeth righteousness at all times.*

4.   The days are evil, and because of it Christians should make the most of their time.

Eph 5:16 *Redeeming the time, because the days are evil.*

5.   Trust the Lord at all times.

Psalms 62:8 *Trust in him at all times; ye people, pour out your heart before him: God is a refuge for us.*

THERE IS A TIME FOR EVERYTHING

1.   There is a wonderful saying about the framework of time on earth. The Ecclesiast declares, *There is a time for every purpose on the earth* and goes on to say that there is a time for birth and death, a time for mourning and dancing, keeping and throwing away, silence and speaking, and there is a time for war and peace.

2.   A key passage for the present time is Ecclesiastes which declares, There is a time for every purpose under heaven. This passage goes on to say that there is a time for birth and death, mourning and dancing, keeping and throwing away, silence and speaking, and war and peace. This is within time.

Eccles 3:1 *To every thing there is a season, and a time to every purpose under the heaven:*

CHAPTER 1

GOD'S SOVEREIGN CONTROL OF TIME

Scripture bears the testimony that God is working out His purposes in man's time. God is working in our present space of time in this world; therefore, the present time is to be used for God's purposes and glory.

1. According to the Bible, the fulfillment of time is an important concept, because it shows God's sovereign control of time in order to bring His promises to pass.
Only God knows the times and seasons for its fulfillment.

Acts 1:7 *And he said unto them, It is not for you to know the times or the seasons, which the Father hath put in his own power.*

1 Thes 5:1 *But of the times and the seasons, brethren, ye have no need that I write unto you.*

2. Preach God's Word.

Titus 1:3 *But hath in due times manifested his word through preaching, which is committed unto me according to the commandment of God our saviour.*

GOD KEEPS HIS PROMISES

Only the Lord knows the times and seasons for the fulfillment of his plans and promises. God has indicated that what He promised long ago would be fulfilled. The fulfillment of time is an important concept because it shows God's sovereign control of time in order to bring His promises to pass.

God promised Abraham that his wife, Sarah, would have a child, and the promise was fulfilled. God told Pharaoh of a plague that would come upon him the next day. God warned Jerusalem that she would be destroyed if His people continued in disobedience and the prophet Jeremiah lamented after their downfall that their time was fulfilled. God fulfilled his promise of a messiah. The birth and death of the Messiah were prophesied in the Old Testament and were fulfilled in the New Testament.

1. The Scripture bears testimony that God is working out His purposes in man's time. He promised Abraham that he and Sarah his wife would have a child.

Gen 18:10 *And he said, I will certainly return unto thee according to the time of life; and, Sarah thy wife shall have a son. And Sarah heard it in the tent door, which was behind him.*

Gen 18:14 *Is any thing too hard for the LORD? At the time appointed I will return unto thee, according to the time of life, and Sarah shall have a son.*

2. God told Pharaoh of a plague that would take place.

Exodus 9:18 *Behold, to morrow about this time I will cause it to rain a very grievous hail, such as hath not been in Egypt since the foundation thereof even until now.*

3. God warned Jerusalem that it would be destroyed if His people continued in disobedience. The Lord hath done that which he had devised; The Bible says the prophet Jeremiah lamented after their downfall that their time was fulfilled.

Lam 2:17 *The LORD hath done that which he had devised; he hath fulfilled his word that he had commanded in the days of old: he hath thrown down, and hath not pitied: and he hath caused thine enemy to rejoice over thee, he hath set up the horn of thine adversaries.*

THE END TIMES

The future and the end times are in God's hands or control. There are many references to the future times which relate to judgment in which Daniel prophesied that the nations will face a time of doom in the future. Israel will also suffer in *the end time of Jacob's trouble.* According to the Bible, during that time many will fall. Nations as well as individuals will face the future time of judgment. The demons realize that they will face a time of torment in the future. The future will not be all doom because in that time Israel will be a restored kingdom. According to the Bible, the future and the end of time are in God's control. According to the Bible the nations will face a time of doom in the future which will be within the time span of God.

Ezek 30:3 *For the day is near, even the day of the LORD is near, a cloudy day; it shall be the time of the heathen.*

1. Daniel had a vision of the end times.

Daniel 8:17 *So he came near where I stood: and when he came, I was afraid, and fell upon my face: but he said unto me, Understand, 0 son of man: for at the time of the end shall be the vision.*

2. The suffering of Israel will be great. However, the future will not be all doom, because in that time Israel will be a restored kingdom and the Messiah will endure forever.

Jer 30:7 *Alas! for that day is great, so that none is like it: it is even the time of Jacob's trouble; but he shall be saved out of it.*

Joel 3:1 *For, behold, in those days, and in that time, when I shall bring again the captivity of Judah and Jerusalem.*

Zeph 3:20 *At that time will I bring you again, even in the time that I gather you: for I will make you a name and a praise among all people of the earth, when I turn back your captivity before your eyes, saith the LORD.*

Daniel 2:44 *And in the days of these kings shall the God of heaven set up a kingdom, which shall never be destroyed: and the kingdom shall not be left to other people, but it shall break in pieces and consume all these kingdoms, and it shall stand for ever.*

3. Nations will also face judgment in the future times.

Psalms 81:15 *The haters of the LORD should have submitted themselves unto him: but their time should have endured for ever.*

Jer 10:15 *They are vanity, and the work of errors: in the time of their visitation they shall perish.*

Matt 24:10 *And then shall many be offended, and shall betray one another, and shall hate one another.*

4. Even demons will face a time of torment.

Matt 8:29 *And, behold, they cried out, saying, What have we to do with thee, Jesus, thou Son of God? art thou come hither to torment us before the time?*

THE KINGDOM OF GOD

The future is in God's hands. This means that the future is filled with fear and uncertainty for the unbelievers but with hope and certainty for believers. The future of unbelievers will be judgment while believers will be exalted by God. The believer eagerly awaits the appointed time of the second coming of the Lord Jesus Christ.

Rev 11:18 *And the nations were angry, and thy wrath is come, and the time of the dead, that they should be judged, and that thou shouldest give reward unto thy servants the prophets, and to the saints, and them that fear thy name, small and great; and shouldest destroy them which destroy the earth.*

1 Pet 5:6 *Humble yourselves therefore under the mighty hand of God, that he may exalt you in due time:*

THE PROMISED MESSIAH

Jesus stated that Israel should have known when the visitation of the Messiah was to take place. His birth and death were prophesied in the Old Testament and were fulfilled in the New Testament. It was also seen in His death at the appointed time. Jesus announced the promised kingdom of God was at hand and continually stated that His hour or time had not yet come; it was to be fulfilled when He was crucified.

1. According to the New Testament, Jesus announced the promised kingdom of God was at hand. We are still talking about things done within the space of time in the world.

Matt 4:17 *From that time Jesus began to preach, and to say, Repent: for the kingdom of heaven is at hand.*

2. Jesus also stated that his time had not yet come.

John 2:4 *Jesus saith unto her, Woman, what have I to do with thee? mine hour is not yet come.*

John 7:6 *Then Jesus said unto them, My time is not yet come: but your time is always ready.*

John 7:8 *Go ye up unto this feast: I go not up yet unto this feast; for my time is not yet full come.*

John 7:30 *Then they sought to take him: but no man laid hands on him, because his hour was not yet come.*

John 8:20 *These words spake Jesus in the treasury, as he taught in the temple: and no man laid hands on him; for his hour was not yet come.*

3. The fulfillment of God's promises can be seen in Christ's death at the appointed time. The first reference is Luke 19:44 in which the visitation was not known.

Luke 19:44 *And shall lay thee even with the ground, and thy children within thee; and they shall not leave in thee one stone upon another; because thou knewest not the time of thy visitation.*

John 12:23 *And Jesus answered them, saying, 'The hour is come, that the Son of man should be glorified.'*

John 13:1 *Now before the feast of the Passover, when Jesus knew that his hour was come that he should depart out of this world unto the Father, having loved his own which were in the world, he loved them unto the end.*

John 17:1 *These words spake Jesus, and lifted up his eyes to heaven, and said, Father, the hour is come; glorify thy Son, that thy Son also may glorify thee:*

4.   The Death of Christ was prophesied. Jesus' death was prophesied in the Old Testament and the fulfillment of this was seen in His death at the appointed time.

Rom 5:6 *For when we were yet without strength, in due time Christ died for the ungodly.*

Gal 4:4 *But when the fullness of the time was come God sent forth his Son, made of a woman made under the law,*

1 Tim 2:6 *Who gave himself a ransom for all, to be testified in due time.*

ETERNITY

Eternity is infinite and unlimited—a time without beginning or end. According Bible scripture, God is portrayed as existing eternally. This is also true with Christ. Unbelievers will face an eternity of punishment. The believer's eternal life begins from the moment of repentance and belief. Believers will live eternally with God in His kingdom.

1.   The future is in God's hands. This means the future is filled with fear and uncertainty for unbelievers, but with hope and certainty for the believer. Believers eagerly await the time of the second coming.

Heb 9:28 *So Christ was once offered to bear the sins of many; and unto them that look for him shall he appear the second time without sin unto salvation.*

Romans 13:11 *And that, knowing the time, that now it is high time to awake out of sleep: for now is our salvation nearer than when we believed.*

2.   According to the Bible, God will exist throughout eternity which means there is no time limit placed on Him.

Exodus 3:14 *And God said unto Moses, I AM THAT I AM: and he said, Thus shalt thou say unto the children of Israel, I AM hath sent me unto you.*

Psalms 90:2 *Before the mountains were brought forth, or ever thou hadst formed the earth and the world, even from everlasting to everlasting, thou art God.*

Rev 1:4 *John to the seven churches which are in Asia: Grace be unto you, and peace, from him which is, and which was, and which is to come; and from the seven Spirits which are before his throne;*

Rev 15:7 *And one of the four beasts gave unto the seven angels seven golden vials full of the wrath of God, who liveth for ever and ever.*

3.   Christ exists throughout eternity as God's son.

Isaiah 9:6 *For unto us a child is born, unto us a son is given: and the government shall be upon his shoulder: and his name shall be called Wonderful, Counselor, The Mighty God, The Everlasting Father, The Prince of Peace.*

John 1:1 *In the beginning was the Word, and the Word was with God, and the Word was God.*

John 1:2 *The same was in the beginning with God.*

John 1:3 *All things were made by him; and without him was not any thing made that was made.*

John 1:18 *No man hath seen God at any time; the only begotten Son, which is in the bosom of the Father, he hath declared him.*

Heb 13:8 *Jesus Christ the same yesterday, and to day, and for ever.*

4. Unbelievers will face an eternity of punishment.

Matt 25:41 *Then shall he say also unto them on the left hand, Depart from me, ye cursed, into everlasting fire, prepared for the devil and his angels:*

Rev 14:11 *And the smoke of their torment ascendeth up for ever and ever: and they have no rest day nor night, who worship the beast and his image, and whosoever receiveth the mark of his name.*

Rev 20:10 *And the devil that deceived them was cast into the lake of fire and brimstone, where the beast and the false prophet are, and shall be tormented day and night for ever and ever.*

John 3:16 *For God so loved the world, that he gave his only begotten Son, that whosoever believeth in him should not perish, but have everlasting life.*

5. Believers will have eternal life through Christ.

John 3:36 *He that believeth on the Son hath everlasting life: and he that believeth not the Son shall not see life; but the wrath of God abideth on him.*

John 5:24 *Verily, verily, I say unto you, He that heareth my word, and believeth on him that sent me, hath everlasting life, and shall not come into condemnation; but is passed from death unto life.*

1 John 5:11 *And this is the record, that God hath given to us eternal life, and this life is in his Son.*

Daniel 7:18 *But the saints of the most High shall take the kingdom, and possess the kingdom for ever, even for ever and ever.*

6. All Dominions shall serve and obey.

Daniel 7:27 *And the kingdom and dominion, and the greatness of the kingdom under the whole heaven, shall be given to the people of the saints of the most High, whose kingdom is an everlasting kingdom, and all dominions shall serve and obey him.*

7. The Lord God will be the light.

Rev 22:5 *And there shall be no night there; and they need no candle, neither light of the sun; for the Lord God giveth them light: and they shall reign for ever and ever.*

Now, according to all we have read thus far, we can understand that although man now lives within a time space frame work, he will live eternally with God who exists eternally and will remove time and space, and man will relate to God in an eternal framework.

ETERNAL GOD

Infinite or unlimited time; is time without beginning or end. The Bible speaks of the eternity of God. As it has been said before, as the creator, God brought the world into being, even before the beginning of time itself. He will also bring the world to its ultimate conclusion, in accordance with His will and purpose.

Isaiah 57:15 *For thus saith the high and lofty One that inhabiteth eternity, whose name is Holy; I dwell in the high and holy place, with him also that is of a contrite and humble spirit, to revive the spirit of the humble, and to revive the heart of the contrite ones.*

Rev 1:4 *John to the seven churches which are in Asia: Grace be unto you, and peace, from him which is, and which was, and which is to come; and from the seven Spirits which are before his throne;*

CHAPTER 2

UNITS OF TIME ESTABLISHED BY GOD

INTRODUCTION

God existed before the world. During creation God defined the framework of time and space and placed man in the world.

Gen 1: 3-5 *And God said, Let there be light: and there was light. And God saw the light, that it was good: and God divided the light from the darkness. And God called the light Day, and the darkness he called Night. And the evening and the morning were the first day.*

Gen 1:14 *And God said, Let there be lights in the firmament of the heaven to divide the day from the night; and let them be for signs, and for seasons, and for days, and years;*

Gen 1:16-18 *And God made two great lights; the greater light to rule the day, and the lesser light to rule the night; he made the stars also. And God set them in the firmament of the heaven to give light upon the earth, And to rule over the day and over the night, and to divide the light from the darkness; and God saw that it was good.*

1.   DAY

The day is divided into three parts: evening, morning and noon.

Ps 55: 1 *Evening and morning, and at noon, will I pray, and say aloud: and he shall hear my voice.*

Midnight was the midpoint of the night.

Matt 25:6 *And at midnight there was a cry made. Behold, the bridegroom cometh; go ye out to meet him.*

In the Old Testament the night was divided into three watches.

Judg 7: 19 *So Gideon, and the hundred men that were with him, came unto the outside of the camp in the beginning of the middle watch; and they had but newly set the watch: and they blew the trumpets, and brake the pitchers that were in their hands.*

Ex 14:24 *And it came to pass, that in the morning watch the LORD looked unto the host of the Egyptians through the pillar of fire and of the cloud, and troubled the host of the Egyptians.*

In the New Testament, the night was divided into four watches.

Matt 14:25 *And in the fourth watch of the night Jesus went unto them, walking on the   sea.*

Mark 13:35 *Watch ye therefore: for ye know not when the master of the house cometh, at even, or at midnight, or at the cockcrowing, or in the morning:*

2.   HOUR

The term hour was used to mean immediately or could express the idea of one-twelfth of daylight.

Dan 3:6 *And whoso falleth not down and worshippeth shall the same hour be cast into the midst of a burning fiery furnace.*

John 11:9 *Jesus answered, are there not twelve hours in the day? If any man walk in the day, he stumbleth not, because he seeth the light of this world.*

3.   WEEK

The week was a seven-day unit begun at the time of creation.

Gen 1:31 *And on the seventh day God ended his work which he had made; and he rested on the seventh day from all his work which he had made.*

The word week means seven.

Gen 29:27 *Fulfill her week, and we will give thee this also for the service which thou salt serve with me yet seven other years.*

Luke 18:12 *I fast twice in the week, I give tithes of all that I possess.*

In Genesis 1:8-31 the days of the week were first, second, third, and so forth.

Gen 1:5-31 *And God called the light Day, and the darkness he called Night. And the evening and the morning were the first day. . .(8) And God called the firmament Heaven. And the evening and the morning were the second day. . .(13) And the evening and the morning were the third day.*

Matt 28:1 *In the end of the Sabbath, as it began to dawn toward the first day of the week, came Mary Magdalene and the other Mary to see the sepulcher.*

4.   SABBATH DAY

The seventh day was known as Sabbath.

Gen 2:2 *And on the seventh day God ended his work which he had made; and he rested on the seventh day from all his work which he had made.*

Ex 16:23 *And he said unto them, This is that which the LORD hath said, Tomorrow is the rest of the holy Sabbath unto the LORD: bake that which ye will bake today, and seethe that ye will seethe; and that which remaineth over lay up for you to be kept until the morning.*

Matt 12:1 *At that time Jesus went on the Sabbath day through the corn; and his disciples were an hungered, and began to pluck the ears of corn, and to eat.*

The day before the Sabbath was called the preparation day and Christians referred to the first day of the week as the Lord's day.

Mark 15:42 *And now when the even was come, because it was the preparation, that is, the day before the Sabbath.*

Rev 1:10 *I was in the Spirit on the Lord's Day, and heard behind me a great voice, as of a trumpet.*

5.   HEBREW NEW YEAR

A Jewish high holy day marks the beginning of the Jewish New Year. The Law of Moses directed that this holiday be observed by *blowing the trumpets*. This festival is also known as the Feast of Trumpets.

6.   MONTH

The month was a unit of time closely tied to the moon. The Hebrew word MON means month. The reason for the connection between the month and the moon is that the beginning of a month was marked by a new moon. The calendar month was about 29 days long. Therefore, the first crescent of the new moon would appear 29 or 30 days after the previous new moon. At times the crescent moon was not visible because of clouds. But this was allowed with a rule that the new moon would never be reckoned as more than 30 days after the last new moon. This prevented too much variation in the calendar.

Deut 33: 14 *And for the precious fruits brought forth by the sun, and for the precious things put forth by the moon.*

CHAPTER 3

TRACKING TIME, SEASONS AND YEARS

The calendar system of reckoning time, usually based on a recurrent natural cycle, such as the sun through the season or the moon; a table, or tabular register of days according to a system usually covering one year and referring to the days of each month to the days of the week.

From the beginning of recorded history the calendar has been used to keep records and predict the time for changing of the seasons. The calendar provided a framework in which man could plan his work. It was an effective timetable for making various religious festivals that were to be celebrated at regular intervals.

DAY

1.   The day is the smallest and most consistent unit of time. In the ancient world, the term day was used in two ways. It described a 24-hour period, as well as day-light in contrast to the night.

2.   The beginning point of the 24-hour day varied. The Bible contains references to the day beginning in the morning; as well as in the evening.

Gen 1:5 *And God called the light Day, and the darkness he called Night. And the evening and the morning were the first day.*

Gen 19:34 *And it came to pass on the morrow, that the firstborn said unto the younger, Behold, I lay yesternight with my father: let us make him drink wine this night also; and go thou in, and lie with him, that we may preserve seed of our Father.*

Act 23:32 *On the morrow they left the horsemen to go with him, and returned to the castle:*

Neh 13: 19 *And it came to pass, that when the gates of Jerusalem began to be dark before the Sabbath, I commanded that the gates should be shut, and charged that they should not be opened till after the Sabbath: and some of my servants set I at the gates, that there should be no burden be brought in on the Sabbath day.*

HOURS

The term hour was used to mean immediately or it could express the idea of one twelfth of daylight.

Dan 3:6 *And whoso falleth not down and worshoppeth shall the same hour be cast into the midst of a burning fiery furnace.*

John 11:9 *Jesus answered, Are there not twelve hours in the day? If any man walk in the day, he stumbleth not, because he seeth the light of this world.*

Daylight was broken into smaller parts.

Ps 55: 17 *Evening, and morning, and at noon, will I pray, and cry aloud: and he shall hear my voice.*

Mark 13:35 *Watch ye therefore: for ye know not when the master of the house cometh, at the even, or at midnight, or at the cockcrowing, or in the morning:*

MORNING AND DAWN

Neh 4:21 *So we labored in the work: and half of them held the spears from the rising of the morning till the stars appeared.*

Ex 14:24 *And it came to pass, that in the morning watch the LORD looked unto the host of Egyptians through the pillar of fire and of the cloud, and troubled the host of Egyptians.*

The Dawn was the twilight before sunrise.

1 Sam 30: 17 *And David smote them from the twilight even unto the evening of the next day: and there escaped not a man of them, save four hundred young men, which rode upon camels, and fled.*

Matt 28:1 *In the end of the Sabbath, as it began to dawn toward the first day of the week, came Mary Magdalene and the other Mary to see the sepulcher.*

NOON AND MIDDAY

Noon was the end of the morning which marked mealtime.

1 King 18:26 *And they took the bullock which was given them, and they dressed it, and called on the name of Baal from morning even until noon, saying, Oh Baal, hear us. But there was no voice, nor any that answered. And they leaped upon the altar which was made.*

Gen 43:16 *And when Joseph saw Benjamin with them, he said to the ruler of his house, Bring these men home, and slay, and make ready: for these men shall dine with me at noon.*

Amos 8:9 *And it shall come to pass in that day, saith the Lord GOD, that I will cause the sun to go down at noon, and I will darken the earth in the clear day:*

Noon was also referred to as midday, broad day-light.

Neh 8:3 *And he read them before the street that was before the water gate from the morning until midday, before the men and the women, and those that could understand; and the ears of all the people were attentive unto the book of the law.*

2 Sam 4:5 *And the sons of Rimmon the Beerothite, Rechab and Baanah, went, and came about the heat of the day to the house of Ishbosheth, who lay on a bed at noon.*

EVENING

The evening was the late afternoon: between the day and the night.

Jer 6:4 *Prepare ye war against her; and let us go up at noon. Woe unto us! For the day goeth away, for the shadows of the evening are stretched out.*

Prov 7:9 *In the twilight, in the evening, in the black and dark night:*

Deut 16:6 *But at the place which the LORD The God shall choose to place his name in, there thou shalt sacrifice the Passover at even, at the going down of the sun, at the season that thou camest forth out of Egypt.*

It could mean literally late in the day.

Mark 11:19 *And when even was come, he went out of the city.*

MIDNIGHT

Matt 25:6 *And at midnight there was a cry made, Behold, the bridegroom cometh; go ye out to meet him.*

Acts 20: 7 *And upon the first day of the week, when the disciples came together to break bread Paul preached unto them, ready to depart on the morrow; and continued his speech until midnight.*

In the Old Testament the night was divided into three watches.

Judg 7: 19 *So Gideon, and the hundred men that were with him, came unto the outside of the camp in the beginning of the middle watch; and they had but newly set watch: and they blew trumpets, and brake pitchers that were in their hands.*

In the New Testament the night was divided into four watches.

Matt 14:25 *And in the fourth watch of the night Jesus went unto them, walking on the sea.*

In the time of the Roman Empire, the day may have begun at midnight, as it is indicated by the Gospel of John.

John 4:6 *Now Jacob's well was there. Jesus therefore, being wearied with his journey, sat thus on the well: and it was about the sixth hour.*

John 19:14 *And it was the preparation of the Passover, and about the sixth hour: and he saith unto the Jews, Behold your King!*

CHAPTER 4

HOLY DAYS AND RELIGIOUS FESTIVALS

HEBREW CALENDAR

In the Old Testament, the marking of time in Old Testament days revolved primarily around the months, seasonal religious festivals, and the year. The month was marked by the first appearance of the crescent of the new moon at sunset. The first day of each month was considered a holy day and required special sacrifices.

First Day of the Month

Num 28:11-13 *And in the beginning of your months ye shall offer a burnt offering unto the LORD; two young bullocks, and one ram, seven lambs of the first year without spot;*
And three tenth deals of flour for a meat offering, mingled with oil, for one bullock; and two tenth deals of flour for a meat offering, mingled with oil, for one ram; And a several tenth deal of flour mingled with oil for a meat offering unto one lamb; for a burnt offering of a sweet savour, a sacrifice made by fire unto the LORD.

A holy day was to be announced with the blowing of trumpets and an offering of special sacrifices.

Num 10:10 *Also in the day of your gladness, and in your solemn days, and in the beginnings of your months, ye shall blow with the trumpets over your burnt offering, and over the sacrifices of your peace offerings; that they may be to you for a memorial before your God: I am the Lord your God.*

Psalms 81:3 *Blow up the trumpet in the new moon, in the time appointed, on our solemn feast day.*

1. Normally the months were designated numerically.

2. According to the writer of the calendar. The first month of the Hebrew calendar was in the spring, around March and April. In their early history the Israelites adopted Canaanite names for the months which were connected with agriculture and climate. Only four of these names are mentioned in the Old Testament: Ziv, the second month; Ethanim, the seventh month; Bul, the eighth month; and Abib, the eleventh month. These four names for the months were associated with the most important times of the year.

First Month of the Hebrew Year

Ex 12:2 *This month shall be unto you the beginning of the months: it shall be the first month of the year to you.*

Second Month: ZIV

Ex 16:1 *And they took their journey from Elim, and all the congregation of the children of Israel came unto the wilderness of Sin, which is between Elim and Sinai, on the fifteenth day of the second month after their departing out of the land of Egypt.*

1 King 6:1 *And it came to pass in the four hundred and eightieth year after the children of Israel were come out of the land of Egypt, in the fourth year of Solomon's reign over Israel, in the month Ziv, which is the second month, that he began to build the house of the LORD.*

1 King 6:37 *In the fourth year was the foundation of the house of the LORD laid, in the month Ziv.*

Third Month:

Ex 19: 1 *In the third month, when the children of Israel were gone forth out of the land of Egypt, the same day came they into the wilderness of Sinai.*

Fourth Month:

2 King 25:3 *And on the ninth day of the fourth month the famine prevailed in the city, and there was no bread for the people of the land.*

Fifth Month:

Jer 28:1 *And it came to pass the same year, in the beginning of the reign of Zedekiah king of Judah, in the fourth year, and in the fifth month, that Hananiah the son of Azur the prophet, which was of Gibelon, spake unto me in the house of the LORD, in the presence of the priests and of all the people,*

Sixth Month:

1 Chr 27:9 *The sixth captain for the sixth month was Ira the son of Ikkesh the Tekoite: and in his course were twenty and four thousand.*

Seventh Month: ETHANIM

Gen 8:4 *And the ark rested in the seventh month, in the seventeenth day of the month, upon the mountains of Ararat.*

The Canaanite word Ethaniam means splendor and refers to the beauty of flowers blooming.

1 King 8:2 *And all the men of Israel assembled themselves unto King Solomon at the feast in the month Ethanim, which is the seventh month.*

Eighth Month: BUL

Zech 1:1 *In the eighth month, in the second year of Darius, came the word of the LORD unto Zechariah, the son of Berechiah, the son of Iddo the prophet,*

The Canaanite name may have referred to rain, since the eighth month was between the early and latter rains.

2 King 7:1 *Then Elisha said, Hear ye the word of the LORD; Thus saith the LORD, To morrow about this time shall a measure of fine flour be sold for a shekel, and two measures of barley for a shekel, in the gate of Samaria.*

Ninth Month:

Ezra 10:9 *Then all the men of Judah and Benjamin gathered themselves together unto Jerusalem within three days. It was the ninth month, on the twentieth day of the month; and all people sat in the street of the house of God, trembling because of this matter, and for the great rain.*

Tenth Month:

Gen 8:5 *And the waters decreased continually until the tenth month, on the first day of the month, were the tops of the mountains seen.*

Eleventh Month: ABIB

Deut 1:3 *And it came to pass in the fortieth year, in the eleventh month, on the first day of the month, that Moses spake unto the children of Israel, according unto all that the LORD had given him in commandment unto them;*

Ex 13:4 *This day came ye out in the month Abib.*

Ex 23:15 *Thou shalt keep the feast of unleavened bread: (thou shalt eat unleavened bread seven days, as I commanded thee, in the time appointed of the month Abib; for in it thou camest out from Egypt: and none shall appear before me empty:*

According to the calendar, this was around the month of March or April, which was at the time barley harvest. The word Abib means ripening of grain.

Lev 2:14 *And if thou offer a meat offering of thy firstfruits unto the LORD, thou shalt offer for the meat offering of thy firstfruits green ears of corn dried by the fire, even corn beaten out of full ears.*

Twelfth Month: ADAR

Esth 3:7 *In the first month, that is, the month Nisan, in the twelfth year of King Ahasuerus, they cast Pur, that is, the lot, before Haman from day to day, and from month to month, to the twelfth month, that is, the month Adar.*

BABYLONIAN CALENDAR

According to the writer in its history the nation of Israel adopted all twelve months of the Babylonian calendar as their civil calendar. All names of all twelve months are not listed in the Bible. Since Israel was an agricultural society, its calendar worked well for the people and their religious festivals.

First Month: NISAN

The first month in the Babylonian calendar also fell during the springtime.

Neh 2:1 *And it came to pass in the month Nisan, in the twentieth year of Artaxerxes the king, that wine was before him and I took up the wine, and gave it unto the king. Now I had not been beforetime sad in his presence.*

Third Month: SIVAN

Esth 8:9 *Then were the king's scribes called at that time in the third month, that is, the month Sivan, on the three and twentieth day thereof; and it was written according to all that Mordecai commanded unto the Jews, and to the lieutenants, and the deputies and rulers of the provinces, according to their language.*

Fifth Month: ELUL

Neh 6:15 *So the wall was finished in the twenty and fifth day of the month Elul, in fifth day of the month Elul, in fifty and two days.*

Ninth Month: CHISLEU

Zech 7:1 *And it came to pass in the fourth year of king Darius, that the word of the LORD came unto Zechariah in the fourth day of the ninth month, even in Chisleu;*

Tenth Month: TEBETH

Esth 2:16 *So Esther was taken unto King Ahasuerus into his house royal in the tenth month, which is the month Tebeth, in the seventh year of his reign.*

Eleventh Month: SEBAT

Zech 1:7 *Upon the four and twentieth day of the eleventh month, which is the month Sebat, in the second year of Darius, came the word of the LORD unto Zechariah, the son Berechiah, the son of Iddo the prophet.*

Twelfth Month: ADAR

Ezra 6:15 *And this house was finished on the third day of the month Adar, which was in the sixth year of the reign of Darius the king.*

HOLY DAYS AND FEASTS

Passover: Feast of Unleavened Bread

In the first month coinciding with our March and April, fourteenth day was Passover.

Ex 12:18 *In the first month, on the fourteenth day of the month at even, ye shall eat unleavened bread, until the one and twentieth day of the month at even.*

The fifteenth day through the twenty first day was unleavened bread.

Lev 23:6 *And on the fifteenth day of the same month is the feast of unleavened bread unto the LORD; even days ye must eat unleavened bread.*

Offering of Firstfruits

The sixteenth day was the firstfruits.

Lev 23:10 *Speak unto the children of Israel, and say unto them, Then ye be come into the land which I give unto you, and shall reap the harvest thereof, then ye shall bring a sheaf of the firstfruits of your harvest unto the priest:*

Lev 23:11 *And he shall wave the sheaf before the LORD, to be accepted for you: on the morrow after the Sabbath the priest shall wave it.*

Lev 23:12 *And ye shall offer that day when ye wave the sheaf an he lamb without blemish of the first year for a burnt offering unto the LORD.*

Lev 23:13 *And the meat offering thereof shall be two tenth deals of fine flour mingled with oil, an offering made by fire unto the LORD for a sweet savour: and the drink offering thereof shall be of wine, the fourth part of an him.*

Lev 23:14 And ye shall eat neither bread, nor parched corn, nor green ears, until the selfsame day that ye have brought an offering unto your God: it shall be a statute for ever throughout your generations in all your dwellings.

Second Month: Passover

Dedicating the first-ripe barley. The second month corresponds to our calendar for April and May, and marked the celebration of a later Passover in case some had missed the first celebration.

Num 9:10 Speak unto the children of Israel, saying, If any man of you or of your posterity shall be unclean by reason of a dead body, or be in a journey afar off, yet he shall keep the Passover unto the LORD.

Num 9:11 The fourteenth day of the second month at even they shall keep it, and eat it with unleavened bread and bitter herbs.

Pentecost: Feast of Weeks

On the sixth day of the second month people celebrate Pentecost, which was also called the Feast of Weeks during the month of May and June.

Lev 23: 15 And ye shall count unto you from the morrow after the Sabbath, from the day that ye brought the sheaf of the wave offering; seven sabbaths shall be complete:

Lev 23:16 Even unto the morrow after the seventh Sabbath shall ye number fifty days; and ye shall offer a new meat offering unto the LORD.

Lev 23:17 Ye shall bring out of your habitations two waves loaves of two tenth deals: they shall be of fine flour; they shall be baked with leaven; they are the firstfruits unto the LORD.

Lev 23: 18 And ye shall offer with the bread seven lambs without blemish of the first year, and one young bullock, and two rams: they shall be for a burnt offering unto the LORD, with their meat offering, and their drink offerings, even an offering made by fire, of the sweet savour unto the LORD.

Lev 23:19 Then ye shall sacrifice one kid of the goats for a sin offering, and two lambs of the first year for a sacrifice of peace offerings.

Lev 23:20 And the priest shall wave them with the bread of the firstfruits for a wave offering before the LORD, with the two lambs: they shall be holy to the LORD for the priest.

Lev 23:21 And ye shall proclaim on the selfsame day, that it may be an holy convocation unto you: ye shall do no servile work therein: it shall be a statute forever in all your dwellings throughout your generations.

Lev 23:22 *And when you reap the harvest of your land, thou shalt not make clean riddance of the corners of thy field when thou reapest, neither shalt thou gather any gleaning of thy harvest: thou shalt leave them unto the poor, and to the stranger. I am the LORD your God.*

Feast of Trumpets

In the seventh month, (September, October) the first day was the Feast of the Trumpets to commemorate the completion of the barley and wheat harvests.

Lev 23:23 *And the Lord spake unto Moses, saying,*

Lev 23:24 *Speak unto the children of Israel, saying, In the seventh month, in the first day of the month, shall ye have Sabbath, a memorial of blowing of trumpets, and an holy convocation.*

Lev 23:25 *Ye shall do no servile work then: but ye shall offer an offering made by fire unto the LORD.*

Day of Atonement

Lev 16:29 *And this shall be a statute forever unto you: that in the seventh month, on the tenth day of the month, ye shall afflict your souls, and do no work at all, whether it be one of your own country, or a stranger that sojourneth among you;*

Lev 16:30 *For on that day shall the priest make an atonement for you, to cleanse you, that ye may be clean from all your sins before the LORD.*

Lev 16:31 *It shall be a Sabbath of rest unto you, and ye shall afflict your souls, by a statute for ever.*

Lev 16:32 *And the priest, whom he shall anoint, and whom he shall consecrate to minister in the priest's office in his father's stead, shall make the atonement, and shall put on the linen clothes, even the holy garments:*

Lev 16:33 *And he shall make an atonement for the holy sanctuary, and he shall make an atonement for the tabernacle of the congregation, and for the altar, and he shall make an atonement for the priests, and for all the people of the congregation.*

Lev 16: 34 *And this shall be an everlasting statute unto you, to make an atonement of the children of Israel for all their sins once a year. And he did as the LORD commanded Moses.*

Feast of the Tabernacles: Feast of Booths

The fifteenth to the twenty-second days were the feast of Tabernacles or ingathering.

Lev 23:33 *And the LORD spake unto Moses, saying,*

Lev 23:34 *Speak unto the children of Israel, saying, The fifteenth day of this seventh month shall be the feast of tabernacles for seven days unto the LORD.*

• The Holy Convocation

Lev 23:35 *On the first day shall be an holy convocation: ye shall do no servile work therein.*

Lev 23:36 *Seven days ye shall offer an offering made by fire unto the LORD: on the eighth day shall be an holy convocation unto you; and ye shall offer an offering made by fire unto the LORD: it is a solemn assembly; and ye shall do no serville work therein.*

• Offerings The Fruit of the Land

Lev 23:37 *These are the feasts of the LORD, which ye shall proclaim to be holy convocations, to offer an offering made by fire unto the LORD, a burnt offering, and a meat offering, a sacrifice, and drink offerings, everything upon his day:*

Lev 23:38 *Beside the Sabbaths of the LORD, and beside your gifts, and beside all your vows, and beside all your freewill offerings, which ye give unto the LORD.*

Lev 23:39 *Also in the fifteenth day of the seventh month, when ye have gathered in the fruit of the land, ye shall keep a feast unto the LORD seven days: on the first day shall be a Sabbath, and on the eighth day shall be a Sabbath.*

• Dwell in a Booth of Boughs

Lev 23:40 *And ye shall take you on the first day the boughs of goodly trees, branches of palm trees, and the boughs of thick trees, and willows of the brook; and ye shall rejoice before the LORD your God seven days.*

Lev 23:41 *And ye shall keep it a feast unto the LORD seven days in the year. It shall be a statute for ever in your generations: ye shall celebrate it in the seventh month.*

Lev 23:42 *Ye shall dwell in booths seven days: all that are Israelites born shall dwell in booths:*

Lev 23:43 *That your generations may know that I made the children of Israel to dwell in booths, when I brought them out of the land of Egypt: I am the LORD your God.*

In commemoration of all the harvests of the year. The feasts revolved around the harvest.

CHAPTER 5

CHRONOLOGY OF CALENDARS

OLD TESTAMENT CALENDAR

The Jewish historian Josephus stated that Israel had two New Years: the commercial New Year, which began in the fall around the seventh month, and the religious New Year, which began in the spring which is the about the first month. Since the months were based on the lunar system and since each month averaged about 29 12 days, the year would be 354 days, or 11 days short of the solar year.

In just three years the calendar would be off more than a month according to the way it was being calculated. To reconcile the lunar month with the solar year, Babylon had a sophisticated system where seven months would be added to the calendar over a 19 year cycle, resulting in an error of only two hours and four minutes by the end of the cycle. This is remarkable accuracy for that day. Israel must have adjusted her calendar in a similar fashion by adding a Second Adar month whenever necessary.

Between the Testaments during the period when the Greeks ruled the ancient world, the seleucid calendar system was most widely used. Two basic Systems were used for reckoning time in the Seleucid era: the Macedonian calendar and the Babylonian calendar. It is difficult to be dogmatic as to which system was used, but the Jewish people seem to have used the Macedonian calendar. This means the Seleucid era in Jewish history began on the first day of their seventh month, Tishri, about 312/311 B. This is according to the Biblical writers.

THE NEW TESTAMENT CALENDAR

The New Testament contains no reference to the Roman or Gentile calendar or to the Jewish calendar, except when speaking of the days of the week.

New Moon

There is one reference to the new moon. (Col 2:16) *Let no man therefore judge you in meat, or in drink, or in respect of an holy day, or of the new moon, or of the Sabbath days:*

The Sabbath

Saturday, is mentioned about 60 times in the New Testament.

• The Disciples Plucked Corn on the Sabbath

Matt 12:1 *At that time Jesus went on the Sabbath day through the corn; and his disciples were an hungered, and began to pluck the ears of corn, and to eat.*

Matt 12:2 *But when the Pharisees saw it, they said unto him, Behold, thy disciples do that which is not lawful to do upon the Sabbath day.*

Matt 12:3 *But he said unto them, Have ye not read what David did, when he was an hungered, and they that were with him;*

Matt 12:4 *How he entered into the house of God, and did eat the shewbread, which was not lawful for him to eat, neither for them which were with him, but only for the priests?*

Matt 12:5 *Or have ye not read in the law, how that on the Sabbath days the priests in the temple profane the Sabbath, and are blameless?*

• Son of Man is LORD

Matt 12:6 *But I say unto you, That in this place is one greater than the temple.*

Matt 12:7 *But if ye had known what this meaneth, I will have mercy, and not sacrifice, ye would not have condemned the guiltless.*

Matt 12:8 *For the Son of man is Lord even of the Sabbath day.*

Matt 12:9 *And when he was departed thence, he went into their synagogue:*

• Jesus Responds to the Pharisees

Matt 12:10 *And, behold, there was a man which had his hand withered. And they asked him, saying, Is it lawful to heal on the Sabbath days? that they might accuse him.*

Matt 12:11 *And he said unto them, What man shall there be among you, that shall have one sheep, and if it fall into a pit on the Sabbath day, will he not lay hold on it, and lift it out?*

Matt 12:12 *How much then is a man better than a sheep? Wherefore it is lawful to do well on the Sabbath days.*

• First Day of the Week: Sunday

Mark 16:2 *And very early in the morning the first day of the week, they came unto the sepulcher at the rising of the sun.*

Luke 24:1 *Now upon the first day of the week, very early in the morning, they came unto the sepulcher, bringing the spices which they had prepared, and certain others with them.*

Acts 20:7 *And upon the first day of the week, when the disciples came together to break bread, Paul preached unto them, ready to depart on the morrow; and continued his speech until midnight.*

1 Cor 16:2 *Upon the first day of the week let every one of you lay by him in store, as God hath prospered him, that there be no gatherings when I come.*

• The Lord's Day: Sunday

Rev 1:10 *I was in the Spirit on the Lord's day and heard behind me a great voice, as of a trumpet,*

• Day of Preparation: Friday

Matt 27:62 *Now the next day, that followed the day of the preparation, the chief priests and Pharisees came together unto Pilate,*

Mark 15:42 *And now when the even was come, because it was the preparation, that is, the day before the Sabbath,*

Luke 23:54 *And that day was the preparation, and the Sabbath drew on.*

John 19:31 *The Jews therefore, because it was the preparation, that the bodies should not remain upon the cross on the Sabbath day, (for that Sabbath day was an high day,) besought Pilate that their legs might be broken, and that they might be taken away.*

John 19:42 *There laid they Jesus therefore because of the Jews' preparation day; for the sepulcher was nigh at hand.*

These are references to the cultic aspects of the Jewish calendar. Frequent mention is made, especially in the Gospel of John, of the Passover.

Passover: A Feast of the Jews

John 2:13 *And the Jews I Passover was at hand, and Jesus went up to Jerusalem,*

John 2:23 *Now when he was in Jerusalem at the Passover, in the feast day, many believed in his name, when they saw the miracles which he did.*

John 6:4 *And the Passover, a feast of the Jews, was nigh.*

John 11:55 *And the Jews Passover was nigh at hand: and many went out of the country up to Jerusalem before the Passover, to purify themselves.*

John 12:1 *Then Jesus six days before the Passover came to Bethany, where Lazarus was which had been dead, whom he raised from the dead.*

John 13:1 *Now before the feast of the Passover, when Jesus knew that his hour was come that he should depart out of this world unto the Father, having loved his own which were in the world, he loved them unto the end.*

John 18:39 *But ye have a custom, that I should release unto you one at the Passover: will ye therefore that I release unto you the King of the Jews?*

FESTIVALS MENTIONED IN THE NEW TESTAMENT

Feast of Unleavened Bread: Passover

Matt 26:17 *Now the first day of the feast of unleavened bread the disciples came to Jesus, saying unto him, Where wilt thou that we prepare for thee to eat the Passover?*

Mark 14:12 *And the first day of unleavened bread, when they killed the Passover, his disciples said unto him, Where wilt thou that we go and prepare that thou mayest eat the Passover?*

Mark 14:1 *After two days was the feast of the Passover, and of unleavened bread: and the chief priests and the scribes sought how they might take him by craft, and put him to death.*

Pentecost

Acts 2:1 *And when the day of Pentecost was fully come, they were all with one accord in one place.*

Acts 20:16 *For Paul had determined to sail by Ephesus, because he would not spend the time in Asia: for he hasted, if it were possible for him, to be at Jerusalem the day of Pentecost.*

1 Cor 16:8 *But I will tarry at Ephesus until Pentecost.*

Feast of the Tabernacles

John 7:2 *Now the Jews/feast of tabernacles was at hand.*

Feast of the Dedication

John 10:22 *And it was at Jerusalem the feast of the dedication, and it was winter.*

REIGNS OF RULERS DENOTE CALENDAR TIME

Although there are no references to the Roman or Gentile calendar in the New Testament, it does refer to the reigns of rulers. There is an example in Luke, which speaks of the fifteenth year of the reign of Tiberius Caesar.

Luke 3:1 *Now in the fifteenth year of the reign of Tiberius Caesar, Pontius Pilate being governor of Judaea, and Herod being tetrarch of Galilee, and his brother Philip tetrarch of Ituraea and of the region of Trachonitis, and Lyeanias the tetrarch of Abilene,*

Luke refers to the time of the rulers then in Judea and the surrounding territories and to the beginning of the ministry of John the Baptist. This must have been in A. D. 28-29, according to the calendar, assuming that Luke used either the Julian calendar, which began in January, or the regal calendar, which began in August. According to Luke, the most general references speak not of the year but of the reigns of emperors Caesar Augustus.

Luke 2:1 *And it came to pass in those days, that there went out a decree from Caesar Augustus, that all the world should be taxed.*

Claudius Caesar

Acts 11:28 *And there stood up one of them named Agabus, and signified by the spirit that there should be great dearth throughout all the world: which came to pass in the days of Claudius Caesar.*

Provincial Governors Quirinius & Gallio

Luke 2:2 *(And this taxing was first made when Cyrenius was governor of Syria.)*

Acts 18:12 *And when Gallio was the deputy of Achaia, the Jews made insurrection with one accord against Paul, and brought him to the judgment seat,*

King Herod

Matt 2: 1 Now when Jesus was born in Bethlehem of Judaea in the days of Herod the king, behold, there came wise men from the east to Jerusalem,

Luke 1:5 There was in the days of Herod, the king of Judaea, a certain priest named Zacharias, of the course of Abia: and his wife was of the daughters of Aaron, and her name was Elisabeth.

Ethnarch Aretas

2 Cor 11:32 *In Damascus the governor under Aretas the king kept the city of the Damascenes with a garrison, desirous to apprehend me:*

PASSOVER

Gospels of Matthew, Mark and Luke

Jesus celebrated Passover with the disciples. The New Testament calendar is that the Gospels of Matthew, Mark, and Luke portray Jesus as having celebrated the Passover with His disciples on the eve of His betrayal.

Matt 26:19 *And the disciples did as Jesus had appointed them; and they made ready the passover.*

Matt 26:20 *Now when the even was come, he sat down with the twelve.*

Luke 22:13 *And they went, and found as he had said unto them: and they made ready the passover.*

Luke 22:14 *And when the hour was come, he sat down, and the twelve apostles with him.*

Luke 22:15 *And he said unto them, With desire I have desired to eat this passover with you before I suffer:*

Gospel of John

The Gospel of John pictures the Jews as not having celebrated the passover at this time.

John 18:28 *Then led they Jesus from Caiaphas unto the hall of judgment: and it was early; and they themselves went not into the judgment hall, lest they should be defiled; but that they might eat the Passover.*

Attempts have been made to reconcile this problem. Possibly, the solution is that the first three gospels reckoned their timetable of the crucifixion events according to the Galilean method beginning the day at sunrise, which was used by Jesus, the disciples, and the Pharisees. But John may have reckoned according to the Judean method (beginning the day at sunset), which is a system used by the Sadducees. If this is true, different calendar systems may have been in use at the same time within the nation of Israel.

UNIT II:
THE
ELECT OF
GOD

The Jews are God's chosen people. Through Christ all classes, races, color and gender of people have become the elect, not only the Jews. Any individual or nation chosen by God is the elect and will take on or assume certain virtues and qualities of Christian life.

Luke 18:7 *And shall not God avenge his own elect, which cry day and night unto him, though he bear long with them.*

CHAPTER 6

CHRISTIAN VIRTUES

Christian virtue, is literally saying to the Christian to take on or assume certain virtues and qualities of a Christian. According to the Bible, Christian standard's for love is God's love in Christ, who died for us. A Christian who sees brethren or sisters in need and shutteth his heart of compassion from him, and does not act to minister to it, there is no love at all. Compassion in one's heart proceeds from our inward care of awareness of others causing us to act in a compassionate way as a Christian in showing Christ-like love.

LOVE OF GOD

1 Jn 3:16 *Hereby perceive we the love of God, because he laid down his life for us: and we ought to lay down our lives for the brethren.*

COMPASSION

1 Jn 3:17 *But whoso hath this world's good, and seeth his brother have need, and shutteth up his bowels of compassion from him, how dwelleth the love of God in him?*

FOREKNOWLEDGE

The Elect ones of God are chosen to salvation according to the foreknowledge of God the Father: Foreknowledge is not simply advance knowledge. It is God's determination in eternity past to bring certain ones into a special relationship with Himself. Peter talked about the Elect according to the foreknowledge of God through the sanctification of the Spirit unto obedience and sprinkling of the blood of Jesus Christ:

1 Pet 1:2 *Elect according to the foreknowledge of God the Father, through sanctification of the Spirit, unto obedience and sprinkling of the blood of Jesus Christ: Grace unto you, and peace, be multiplied.*

OBEDIENCE

1.   In Peter 1:2 we see the sanctification of the Spirit, unto obedience and sprinkling of the blood of Jesus Christ: We understand the Spirit is set apart for salvation from destruction of those whom God has foreknown.

2.   Sprinkling of the blood is an allusion to Exodus 24 in which the blood was sprinkled on the altar as a symbol of the people's obedience as to what verse 2 here is saying about the Spirit, unto obedience. In Exodus it was also on the people as a symbol of God's acceptance.

Ex 24:4 *And Moses wrote all the words of the LORD, and rose up early in the morning, and builded an altar under the hill, and twelve pillars, according to the twelve tribes of Israel.*

Ex 24: 5 *And he sent young men of the children of Israel, which offered burnt offerings, and sacrificed peace offerings of oxen unto the LORD.*

Ex 24:6 *And Moses took half of the blood, and put it in basins; and half of the blood he sprinkled on the altar.*

Ex 24:7 *And he took the book of the covenant, and read in the audience of the people: and they said, All that the LORD hath said will we do, and be obedient.*

Ex 24:8 *And Moses took the blood, and sprinkled it on the people, and said, Behold the blood of the covenant, which the LORD hath made with you concerning all these words.*

3.   According to James who is addressing Christian readers, any one my stray and commit sin. He is not speaking of saving someone per say, but to restore them to the path of obedience. Only God can restore a soul or life spiritually.

James 5:19 *Brethren, if any of you do err from the truth, and one convert him;*

James 5:20 *Let him know, that he which converteth the sinner from the error of his way shall save a soul from death, and shall hide a multitude of sins.*

FORBEARANCE AND FORGIVENESS

1.   The fact that believers are being urged to assume the virtues of forbearing and forgiving one another as Col 3:12 instructs us to do, signifies that none has yet arrived to that point spiritually. We don't seem to be able to do that.

2.   As believers develop these virtues, we must be forbearing and forgiving toward our fellow church members. Our Christian brother is also in the process of acquiring these virtues. This verse is significant because it seems that some of us are still holding onto our flaws and weakness. This shows that some of us need to be a little more forbearing and forgiving.

Because we are the elect of God, we should be the elect of God in deed and thought also. We are to be obedient and forgiving. This is what Christian virtues is all about.

Col 3: 12 *Put on therefore, as the elect of God, holy and beloved, bowels [hearts] of mercies, kindness, humbleness of mind, meekness, longsuffering;*

Col 3:13 *Forbearing one another, and forgiving one another, if any man have a quarrel against any: even as Christ forgave you, so also do ye.*

1 Pet 1:2 *Elect according to the foreknowledge of God the Father, through sanctification of the Spirit, unto obedience and sprinkling of the blood of Jesus Christ: Grace unto you, and peace, be multiplied.*

Mark 11:25 *And when ye stand praying, forgive, if ye have ought against any: that your Father also which is in heaven may forgive you your trespasses.*

KINDNESS

Being kind and tenderhearted brings about charity which is love and the bond of perfection.

Eph 4:32 *And be ye kind one to another, tenderhearted, forgiving one another, even as God for Christ's sake hath forgiven you.*

CHARITY

Love is the crowning grace completing the Christian virtues required for perfectness or being as God's elect people. Look at what Christian's virtues will do for the believer or God's elect people. As a bond it binds all other virtues of a Christian together in harmony and unity.

Col 3:14 *And above all these things put on charity, which is the bond of perfectness.*

1 Cor 13:4 *Charity suffereth long, and is kind; charity envieth not; charity vaunteth not itself, is not puffed up.*

CHAPTER 7

SIN AND PUNISHMENT

God punishes his disobedient people and sometimes it is with death. The story of Ananias in Acts 5:5-10 is often quoted to prove that point. Since we are under grace that really doesn't apply. However, we should look more into it for better understanding of the word of God.

TEMPTATION

1. Ananias sold a possession and kept back part of the price and brought it to the apostles. The apostle Peter rebuked him saying, *thou has not lied unto men, but unto God* (Acts 5.4).

Acts 5.5 And Ananias hearing these words fell down, and gave up the ghost: and great fear came on all them that heard these things.

2. God does not judge every believer with death. Now that we are under grace and a better covenant, the love of God has made it possible for the believer to repent for the disobedience and sin.

3. Ananias and his wife lied to the Spirit and to the man of God, and because of it they paid with their lives.

1 Cor 10:9 *Neither let us tempt Christ, as some of them also tempted, and were destroyed of serpents.*

1 Cor 10:11 *Now all these things happened unto them for examples: and they are written for our admonition, upon whom the ends of the world are come.*

1 Cor 10: 12 *Wherefore let him that thinketh he standeth take heed lest he fall.*

1 Cor 10:13 *There hath no temptation taken you but such as is common to man: but God is faithful, who will not suffer you to be tempted above that ye are able; but will with the temptation also make a way to escape, that ye may be able to bear it.*

BIBLICAL EXAMPLES THAT TEACH

1.   These biblical examples were written for our admonition. Paul wrote in Romans 15:4, *For whatsoever things were written aforetime were written for our learning, that we through patience and comfort of the scriptures might have hope.*

2.   The example of Ananias and his wife is given to us as an example. The death that came upon them as punishment was to teach us that there are penalties for our actions.

Acts 2:5 *Great fear came upon all the church, and upon as many as heard these things.*

THE LAW CONCERNING VOWS

1.   Ananias and his wife knew the law and the teachings about breaking a vow made to a person and even unto God. The principle is that God cannot break His word.
God gave Moses a command to give to the children of Israel.

Num 30:2 *If a man make a vow unto the Lord or swear an oath to bind his soul with a bond he shall not break it.*

2.   Ananias's wife knew she was wrong. Peter asked her if she kept back some of the money and she said yes. She and her husband agreed to the matter it seems. They keep the vow they made with each other, yet forgot the vow made to the church and to God.

3.   The word of God had to be kept in order for the people to believe God will do the things He says He will do. So again, God doesn't always judge sin with instant death. With Ananias and his wife, it was done to put fear upon the people (Acts 5:11).

4.   Reading and studying the Bible helps us better understand the ways of God. He tells us what He wants us to do in order to please Him. Look at Ananias and his wife. If a man or woman makes a vow unto the Lord, or binds themselves by a bond, their vows shall stand. Ananias made a vow unto the church and to the apostle. Ananias and his wife lied to the people and before God.

Num 30:2 *If a man make a vow to the LORD, or swear an oath to bind his soul with a bond; he shall not break his word, he shall do according to all that proceedeth out of his mouth.*

There are two types of vows: one, the vow (neder) and the vow that bonds (issar).

1.   Neder is a vow that is more commonly used and is a law we are commanded to keep. The action would be to do something positive such as offering a sacrifice.

2.   Issar is a self-imposed vow.

Ps 132:2 *How he sware unto the LORD, and vowed unto the mighty God of Jacob;*

Ps 132:3 *Surely I will not come into the tabernacle of my house, nor go up into my bed;*

Ps 132:4 *I will not give sleep to mine eyes, or slumber to mine eyelids,*

Ps 132:5 *Until I find out a place for the LORD, an habitation for the mighty God of Jacob.*

3. We cannot substitute self-imposed religious obligations for God given duties.

4. A vow made by a woman could be invalidated by her father or her husband.

Num 30:4 *And her father hear her vow, and her bond wherewith she hath bound her soul, and her father shall hold his peace at her: then all her vows shall stand, and every bond wherewith she had bound her soul shall stand.*

Num 30:7 *And her husband hear it, and held his peace at her in the day that he heard it: then her vows shall stand, and her bonds wherewith she bound her soul shall stand.*

Num 30:8 *But if her husband disallowed her on the day that he heard it; then he shall make her vow which she vowed, and that which she uttered with her lips, wherewith she bound her soul, of none effect; and the Lord shall forgive her.*

Num 30:9 *But every vow of a widow, and of her that is divorced, wherewith they have bound their souls, shall stand against her.*

5. A wife's duty to submit to her husband was comparable to the child's duty to obey his parents as in Numbers 30:3-5. Neither wives nor children could substitute self-imposed religious obligations for God given duties.

6. Ananias and his wife did indeed break their vows to God by keeping back some of the money which was for the work of God. Their voluntary pledge to sell the land and give the money to the church was a religious obligation (vow) they made to the group and to God.

CHAPTER 8

UNITY OF THE SPIRIT

Ananias and his wife were a part of a group that had received the Holy Spirit. As believers, they had many things in common through unity of the spirit.

UNITY OF SPIRIT

Acts 4:31 *And when they had prayed, the place was shaken where they were assembled together; and they were all filled with the Holy Ghost, and they spake the word of God with boldness.*

Eph 4:2,3. *With all lowliness and meekness, with longsuffering, forbearing one another in love; endeavoring to keep the unity of the Spirit in the bond of peace.*

Being of the Same Mind

This shows how the unity of the spirit can and will be with us if we are all of one heart and one soul, there can the witness of the resurrection of Christ be seen in us.

Acts 4:32 *And the multitude of them that believed were of one heart and of one soul: neither said any of them that ought of the things which he possessed was his own; but they had all things common.*

Receiving Power and Grace

Acts 4:33 *And with great power gave the apostles witness of the resurrection of the Lord Jesus: and great grace was upon them all.*

Sharing Possessions

1. This is showing the elect of God having the same mind and assuming certain virtues and qualities of a Christian.

Acts 4:34 *Neither was there any among them that lacked: for as many as were possessors of lands or houses sold them, and brought the prices of the things that were sold,*

Acts 4:35 *And laid them down at the apostles' feet: and distribution was made unto every man according as he had need.*

2.   When you have hearts of mercy, kindness, and humbleness toward others you can obey the word of God coming from your pastor, when he asks you to help in giving to the church.

Joining God's Family

At one time we were all without Christ. Through Christ we are no longer strangers.

Eph 2:11 *Wherefore remember, that ye being in time past Gentiles in the flesh, who are called Uncircumcised by that which is called the Circumcision in the flesh made by hands;*

Eph 2:12 *That at that time ye were without Christ, being aliens from the commonwealth of Israel, and strangers from the covenants of promise, having no hope, and without God in the world:*

Eph 2:19 *Now therefore ye are no more strangers and foreigners, but fellow citizens with the saints, and of the household of God;*

Building on the Foundation of Christ

Eph 2:20 *And are built upon the foundation of the apostles and prophets, Jesus Christ himself being the chief comer stone;*

Eph 2:21 *In whom all the building fitly framed together groweth unto an holy temple in the Lord:*

Eph 2:22 *In whom ye also are builded together form a habitation of God through the Spirit.*

GOD'S GRACE IS OUR SALVATION

The grace of God is the expression of His goodness toward the undeserving. Since Christ died for the sins of the world, grace could mean, God's (riches at Christ's expense). This grace is the basis of our salvation.

Ph 1:7 *In whom we have redemption through his blood, the forgiveness of sins, according to the riches of his grace;*

Ph 2:8 *For by grace are ye saved through faith; and that not of yourselves: it is the gift of God:*

WALKING IN THE SPIRIT

When you walk in the spirit you will experience a change in your behavior as you yield to the Spirit. Christ's life will manifest in the believer's life as fruit of the Spirit and a life following the teachings of Christ and not of the law.

Delight in the Law of God

Eph 1:4 *God has chosen us in him before the foundation of the world, that we should be holy and without blame before him in love.*

The law works by compulsion from without; grace works by compassion from within.
The Christian does not need the restraints of the law because his moral life is governed by the Spirit of God.

Ga 15:18 *But if ye be led of the Spirit, ye are not under the law.*

Rom 7:22 *For I delight in the law of God after the inward man.*

Live by the Spirit

To live by the Spirit: Christians are to rely on the Spirit's help. The question is how does one live by the Spirit?

1. The Christian must believe the Spirit is with him, having been sent by God into his heart.

Eph 4:6 *One God and Father of all, who is above all, and through all, and in you all.*

2. In every spiritual confrontation the believer must yield to the Spirit, that is, submit our own desires to those of the Spirit. We must depend on the Spirit for help, enabling us to live a God pleasing life
Gal 4:5 *To redeem them that were under the law, that we might receive the adoption of sons.*

3. The believer who lives by the Spirit will not error or sin as a result of lust which is strong desires of the flesh and the sinful nature of man.

Gal 5:16 *This I say then, Walk in the Spirit, and ye shall not fulfill the lust of the flesh.*

Yield to the Spirit

1. The Holy Spirit and the sinful nature of man's physical desires and yearnings are contrary to each other. The Christian finds himself a battlefield of his desires to do good and evil. The outcome of it is that believers cannot do the things they want.

Gal 5: 17 *For the flesh lusteth against the Spirit, and the Spirit against the flesh: and these are contrary the one to the other: so that ye cannot do the things that ye would.*

2. We have the desire to do the will of God in our hearts, but because of our own will, we become captive to our sinful nature when we give in to our lusts.

Rom 7:18 *For I know that in me (that is, in my flesh,) dwelleth no good thing: for to will is present with me; but how to perform that which is good I find not.*

Rom 7:22 *For I delight in the law of God after the inward man:*

Rom 7:23 *But I see another law in my members, warring against the law of my mind, and bringing me into captivity to the law of sin which is in my members.*

3.   It would seem that the believer is caught in a hopeless tug-of-war between the flesh and the Spirit. However, that is not the case because God has given us the solution. When Christians yield to the spirit, they are then led by it. When we yield to the Spirit, we will turn from the flesh's evil yearning and remove sin from our daily lives.

Rom 6:4 *Therefore we are buried with him by baptism unto death; that like as Christ was raised up from the dead by the glory of the Father, even so we also should walk in newness of life.*

Rom 6:5 *For if we have been planted together in the likeness of his death, we shall be also in the likeness of his resurrection.*

Become Servants of Righteousness

1.   Sin will not have dominion over believers, because they are no longer under the law, but under grace.

Rom 6:14 *For sin shall not have dominion over you: for ye are not under the law, but under grace.*

Rom 6:18 *Being then made free from sin, ye became the servants of righteousness.*

Rom 6:22 *But now being made free from sin, and become servants to God, ye have your fruit unto holiness, and the end everlasting life.*

2.   Just because we are under grace isn't saying that we are to sin.

Rom 6:15 *What then? Shall we sin, because we are not under the law, but under grace? God forbid.*

3.   We are servants to those we serve, so we must choose whether we are to be servants to sin or to righteousness.

Rom 6:16 *Know ye not, that to whom ye yield yourselves servants to obey, his servants ye are to whom ye obey; whether of sin unto death, or of obedience unto righteousness?*

4.   Furthermore, we should be ashamed of ourselves when we sin, for there are no fruit of the Spirit in a sinful person.

Rom 6:21 *What fruit had ye then in those things whereof ye are now ashamed? For the end of those things is death.*

The phrase when being led means there is an indication of submission; whether it is to the Spirit or to sinful flesh. The believer decides by whom he will be led and it can be either by his flesh or by the Spirit.

BURIED WITH CHRIST BY BAPTISM

1. We are buried with Christ by baptism from his death; and as Christ was raised from the dead by the glory of the Father, so are we. Therefore, we are to walk in the newness of life.

Rom 6:4 *Therefore we are buried with him by baptism into death: that like as Christ was raised up from the dead by the glory of the Father, even so we also should walk in newness of life.*

2. Walking in the newness of life is saying that the believer is to be alive in the Spirit, because we are crucified with him, and the body of sin is dead.

Rom 6:6 *Knowing this, that our old man is crucified with him, that the body of sin might be destroyed, that henceforth we should not serve sin.*

3. Now that we are planted together in his likeness we are to be in the likeness of his resurrection from the dead.

Rom 6:5 *For if we have been planted together in the likeness of his death, we shall be also in the likeness of his resurrection*

4. Now that we have been made free from sin, we are servants to God.

Rom 6:22 *But now being made free from sin, and become servants to God, ye have your fruit unto holiness, and the end everlasting life.*

5. Sin is not to reign in our mortal body and we should not obey the list of the flesh.

Rom 6: 12 *Let not sin therefore reign in your mortal body, that ye should obey it in the lusts thereof.*

6. As Servants of righteousness we yield to the Spirit of truth and righteousness.

Rom 6:18 *Being then made free from sin, ye became the servants of righteousness.*

FRUIT OF THE SPIRIT

By comparing the works of the flesh with the fruit of the Spirit, a person can readily see whether he is walking by the Spirit or being controlled by the flesh.

Rom 6:22 *But now being made free from sin, and become servants to God, ye have your fruit unto holiness, and the end everlasting life.*

Rom 6:21 *What fruit had ye then in those things whereof ye are now ashamed? For the end of those things is death.*

Fruit from Works of the Flesh

Galations 5:20-21 concerning the results of the fruit really spells it out. There is no doubt whether an individual is living by the Spirit or not.

Gal 5:19 *Now the works of the flesh are manifest, which are these; Adultery, fornication, uncleanness, lasciviousness,*

Gal 5:20 *Idolatry, witchcraft, hatred, variance, emulations, wrath, strife, seditions, heresies,*

Gal 5:21 *Envyings, murders, drunkenness, revellings, and such like: of the which I tell you before, as I have also told you in time past, that they which do such things shall not inherit the kingdom of God.*

Idolatry. According to Bible scripture, idolatry is not just the worship of graven images, it can also mean putting one's affections or efforts on a thing or a person instead of putting it on God.

Witchcraft and Sorcery. Witchcraft is sorcery, that is, tampering with the power of evil. According to the way man sees it, it is or could include dabbling in the occult.

Variance. Variance is strife, discord, and disagreement .

Emulations. Emulations means ambition or endeavor. It can also mean jealousy or strife. Strife can be selfish ambition which is saying a person who is selfish is one who is controlled by their ambition, strong desirous, and possession.

Seditions are dissensions. A person who causes an insurrection or discontent against the government, or of resistance to the lawful authority.

Heresies are permanent, organized divisions, which is in the church. Heresies are a religious opinion opposed to the authorized doctrinal standards of any particular church.

Avoid Evil

Whereas Ephesians 5 speaks of living the life of love, Eph 5:3 it speaks of uncleanliness or covetousness and Eph 5:11 tells us to have no fellowship with the unfruitful works of darkness.

Eph 5:3 *But fornication, and all uncleanness, or covetousness, let it not be once named among you, as becometh saints;*

Eph 5:11 *And have no fellowship with the unfruitful works of darkness, but rather reprove them.*

FRUIT OF THE HOLY SPIRIT

In contrast to the works of the flesh which we are capable of performing, the fruit of the Holy Spirit is given only by God. Christian character should result from Christ living in them.

Gal 5:22 *But the fruit of the Spirit is love, joy, peace, longsuffering, gentleness, goodness, faith,*

Gal 5:23 *Meekness, temperance: against such there is no law.*

Gal 2:20 *I am crucified with Christ: nevertheless I live; yet not I, but Christ liveth in me: and the life which I now live in the flesh I live by the faith of the Son of God, who loved me, and gave himself for me.*

Maturity of Spirit

In order for Christ to develop in the believer all of the aspects of the spirit or fruit of the Holy Spirit must mature. The character of Christ is the fullest manifestation of the fruit of the spirit in the New Testament. Jesus did not recognize the traditions of men; His enemies were unable to prove any charge against Him.

James 1:5 *If any of you lack wisdom, let him ask of God, that giveth to all men liberally, and upbraideth not; and it shall be given him.*

Ex 35:31 *And he hath filled him with the spirit of God, in wisdom, in understanding, and in knowledge, and in all manner of workmanship;*

Gal 5:23 *Meekness, temperance: against such there is no law.*

Phil 1:6 *Being confident of this very thing, that he which hath begun a good work in you will perform it until the day of Jesus Christ:*

The Royal Law

If you fulfill the royal law you will love your neighbor as yourself, and if you do that you will do well according to the Bible.

James 2:8 *If ye fulfill the royal law according to the scripture, Thou shalt love thy neighbour as thyself, ye do well:*

Wisdom

James 1:5 *If any of you lack wisdom, let him ask of God, that giveth to all men liberally, and upbraideth not; and it shall be given him.*

James 1:6 *But let him ask in faith, nothing wavering. For he that wavereth is like a wave of the sea driven with the wind and tossed.*

James 1:7 *For let not that man think that he shall receive any thing of the Lord.*

James 1: *A double minded man is unstable in all his ways.*

James 1:26 *If any man among you seem to be religious, and bridleth not his torque, but deceiveth his own heart, this man 's religion is vain.*

CHAPTER 9

PARENTS AND CHILDREN

Parents have a great responsibility to raise their children to be followers of Christ and loving servants of the Lord. Respect and love flow both ways, just as our love for Jesus and his love for us.

Eph 6:1 *Children obey your Parents in the Lord: for this is right.*

1.   In the Lord does not modify parents, for this would mean that only Christian parents are to be obeyed. Rather it goes with obey, that is, obey those parental instructions whether from Christian or none Christian parents that are in line with the Lord's will.

2.   Honor is having that respect inwardly and outwardly.

Eph 6:2 *Honor thy father and mother; which is the first commandment with promise.*

3.   Exodus 20: 3-17 are the Ten Commandments God has given us. Verse 12 is the fifth commandment. While it commands children to honor their parents, it is the first of God's Old Testament injunctions to be given that possesses an attached Promise.

Ex 20:12 *Honor thy father and thy mother: that thy days may be long upon the land which the Lord thy God giveth thee.*

4. The Promise is twofold: honoring and obeying parents (i) ensures a long and (ii) prosperous life upon the earth.

Eph 6:2 *Honour thy father and mother; (which is the first commandment with promise;)*

Eph 6:3 *That it may be well with thee, and thou mayest live long on the earth.*

PARENTAL RESPONSIBILITIES AND DUTIES

Basically, we are to spiritually educate and admonish. This means that we need to point out one's responsibilities and duties. Of the Lord is in Greek and is a subjective qenitive. This indicates that behind the parents' teaching and instructing their children that the Lord is the chief teacher in a child's education. Parents do not rear their children alone.

SPECIAL REMINDER TO FATHERS

Eph 6:4 *And, ye fathers, provoke not your children to wrath: but bring them up in the nurture and admonition of the Lord.*

INSTRUCTION TO SERVANTS

Eph 6:5-9
Obey them that are your master. Not with eye service, as menpleasers.
With good will doing service as to the Lord. Knowing whatsoever good thing you do shall be receive of the Lord. And masters, do the same thing unto them.

CHAPTER 10

THE ARMOR OF GOD

PREPARE FOR SPIRITUAL WARFARE

The Apostle Paul said, *finally, my brethren, be strong in the Lord* (Eph 6:10).

One could look at this as to say, from now on or henceforth. The Spiritual battle of the Christians life in which they are engaged will exist from now on until the coming of the Lord's return for His people:

Eph 6:10 *Finally, my brethren, be strong in the Lord, and in the power of his might.*

There is a sense of urgency demanding immediate action. The believer is in warfare with the different spirits, but must he stand firm and steadfast. The military overtone was used in classical Greek meaning to resist the enemy and hold a position in battle.
The wiles of the devil or Devil's are Satan who carefully devises and tactics against believers.

Eph 6:11 *Put on the whole armor of God that we may be able to stand against the wiles of the devil.*

In 2 Corinthians 6:7 Paul wrote about having the armor of righteousness on the right hand and the left. The armor or righteousness is the word of truth. Paul talked about the hidden things of dishonesty: Not walking in craftiness and not handling the word of God deceitfully; but rather by the manifestation of the truth. Paul is preaching the truth which is the word of God.

2 Cor 6:7 *By the word of truth by the power of God, by the armor of righteousness on the right hand and on the left.*

2 Cor 4:2 *But have renounced the hidden things of dishonesty, not walking in craftiness, nor handling the word of God deceitfully: but by manifestation of the truth commending ourselves to every man's conscience in the sight of God.*

ACTIVITIES OF DEMONS

1.   The Bible speaks of demons. Sometimes they cause physical disease or mental suffering. Not all mental disorders are demonic. Demons also tempt people into immoral practices.

Mark 1:23 *And there was in their synagogue a man with an unclean spirit; and he cried out.*

2.   They originate and propagate false doctrines taught by religious groups. The Bible speaks of them as being in high places.

Eph 6:12 *For we wrestle not against flesh and blood, but against principalities, against powers, against the rulers of the darkness of this world, against spiritual wickedness in high places.*

3.   The Bible says sometimes people are possessed by demons. Even though demons are committed to do evil, God will use them to accomplish His plan during the end of the age.

1 Tim 4:1 *Now the Spirit speaketh expressly, that in the latter times some shall depart from the faith, giving heed to seducing spirits, and doctrines of devils:*

SPIRITUAL WARFARE

1.   The expression of being engaged in hand to hand combat emphasizes the personal individual nature of spiritual warfare waged against local church and Christians.

Rev 16: 14 *For they are the spirits of devils, working miracles, which go forth unto the kings of the earth and of the whole world, to gather them to the battle of that great day of God Almighty.*

2.   Flesh and blood seem to refer to humanity according to the Bible. Flesh and blood is not the church's adversary. Instead she opposes principalities. Principalities are rulers and powers of authorities who have succumbed to spiritual wickedness. Wicked spiritual beings are fallen angels such as demons and Lucifer himself.

Eph 6:12 *For we wrestle not against flesh and blood, but against principalities, against powers, against the rulers of the darkness of this world, against spiritual wickedness in high places.*

PREPARE FOR THE ATTACK

1.   Because we are facing spiritual evil and wickedness, we must put on the whole armor of God that we might be able to withstand the attack. We must have the armor God has provided to help the believers who trust Him. Otherwise the enemy will destroy our Christian witness and ministry. Evil days are the times that we are faced with now, people who are doing things which are Satanic, the devil.

2.   Having done all to stand includes both, dressing oneself in the armor and resisting Satan. Having done all we can to prepare, the Devil will attack again & again. Understanding this will help to clarify Ephesians 6:12. Christian witness and ministry verse 13.

Eph 6:13 *Wherefore take unto you the whole armor of God that ye may be able to withstand in the evil day and having done all to stand.*

THE ARMOR OF GOD

The whole armor of God consists of six pieces. (Eph. 6:14-21)

1.   Belt of Truth. Having your lions girt about with the truth consist of the word of God. Ancient soldiers wore a leather belt at their waist which held most of the other pieces of his armor in place. Similarly a Christian's armor is held in place by a spiritual belt or his knowledge of the truth of the Scripture.

Eph 6:14 *Stand therefore, having your loins girt about with truth, and having on the breastplate of righteousness;*

2 Cor 6:7 *By the word of truth, by the power of God; by the armor of righteousness on the right hand and on the left,*

Isaiah 11:5 *Righteousness shall be the girdle of his loins, and faithfulness the girdle of this reins.*

2.   *Breastplate*. The breastplate is righteousness. It represents a holy character and moral conduct. Obedience to the truth which is known to produce a godly life of righteousness. (Eph. 6:14)

Isaiah 59:17 *For he put on righteousness as a breastplate, and an helmet of salvation upon his head: and he put on the garments of vengeance for clothing, and was clad with zeal as a cloak.*

3.   *Footwear*. Eagerness that comes from the gospel of peace. This is similar to the Roman soldiers who wore special hobnailed sandals called caligae which enabled the soldier to advance against his enemy. The Christian must have on his feet a sense of eagerness or willingness to advance against the Devil and take the fight to him. Such eagerness to contend with Satan comes from the gospel of peace. The gospel gives peace to the believer, freeing and helping to advance against such powerful opponent.

Eph. 6:15 *And your feet shod with the preparation of the gospel of peace;*

4.   *Shield*. The shield is the shield of faith. In other words, take God at His word by believing in His Promises. Such trust will protect one from doubts induced by Satan.

Eph. 6:16 *Above all, taking the shield of faith, wherewith ye shall be able to quench all the fiery darts of the wicked.*

Eph 2:8 *For by grace are ye saved through faith; and that not of yourselves: it is the gift of God:*

Isaiah 52:7 *How beautiful upon the mountains are the feet of him that bringeth good tidings, that publisheth peace; that bringeth good tidings of good, that publisheth salvation; that saith unto Zion. Thy God reigneth!*

5. **Helmet**. The helmet is salvation. According to the Bible the readers are already Christians and need not to be saved. The Thessalonians describes this helmet the help of salvation that is the certainty (assurance of salvation).

Eph. 6:17 *And take the helmet of salvation, and the sword of the Spirit, and watching thereunto with all perseverance and supplication for all saints;*

1 Thes 5:8 *But let us who are of the day be sober putting on the breastplate of faith and love: and for an helmet the hope of salvation.*

6. **Sword**. The sword of the Spirit is the word of God. The Greek term rendered word is not logos referring to the whole word of God but rhema referring to certain portions or selected verses of Scripture. Reference taken from verses 14 through 17.

STEADFAST IN THE LOVE OF GOD

Romans 8:38 *For I am Persuaded, that neither death, nor life, nor angels, nor Principalities, nor Powers, nor things present nor things to come,*

Romans 8:39 *Nor height nor depth, nor any other creature, shall be able to separate us from the love of God, which is in Christ Jesus our Lord.*

REVENGE DISOBEDIENCE

2 Cor 10:4 *For the weapons of our warfare are not carnal, but mighty through God to the Pulling down of strong holds.*

2 Cor 10:5 *Casting down imaginations, and every high thing that exalteth itself against the knowledge of God, and bringing into captivity every thought to the obedience of Christ;*

2 Cor 10:6 *And having in a readiness to revenge all disobedience when your obedience is fulfilled.*

VICTORY

1 John 5:4 *For whatsoever is born of God overcometh the world: and this is the victory that overcometh the world, even our faith.*

CHAPTER 11

THE SIGNIFICANCE OF GOD'S WISDOM

The biblical concept of wisdom is quite different from the classical view of the wisdom, which is sought through the philosophy of man's rational thoughts to determine the mysteries of the existences and the universe.

The first principle of biblical wisdom is that man should humble himself before God in reverence and worship, and be obedient to His commands. This is found especially in the books of Job, Psalms, Proverbs, and Ecclesiastes which are the wisdom literature.

To follow the best course of action, based on knowledge and understanding, that which is against the wisdom of God is in contrast to the wisdom of man, which is the wisdom of this world, human wisdom.

1 Cor 2:4 *And my speech and my preaching was not with enticing words of man's wisdom, but in demonstration of the Spirit and of power;*

1 Cor 2:5 *That your faith should not stand in the wisdom of men, but in the power of God.*

1 Cor 2:6 *Howbeit we speak wisdom among them that are perfect: yet not the wisdom of this world, nor of the princes of this world, that come to nought;*

1 Cor 2:9 *But as it is written, Eye hath not seen, or ear heard, neither have entered into the heart of man, the things which God hath prepared for them that love him.*

1 Cor 2:13 *Which things also we speak, not in the words which man's wisdom teacheth, but which the Holy Ghost teacheth; comparing spiritual things with spiritual.*

According to 1 Corinthians 2:5 and verse 9, there are things man has not seen, heard, neither have they entered into the heart of man, the things which God had prepared for them that love Him.

Additional Reference: Isaiah 64:4-12;
Psalms 31:19-24; Psalms 27:13,14; Isaiah 25:9; and the wisdom of man (1 Corinthians 2:5).

WISDOM IS GOD'S GIFT

1. In 1 Corinthians 2:2, Paul gave careful thought to his approach to lay aside the philosophical skill to announce Jesus Christ who was crucified. This message reflected divine wisdom.

1 Cor 2:2 *For I determined not to know any thing among you, save Jesus Christ, and him crucified.*

2. In 1 Cor 2:4 it seems that the Corinthians thought they knew a great deal about the Holy Spirit. More than most churches in the apostolic times, it seems that they had experienced various of the manifestations of the Spirit's power.

1 Cor 2:4 *And my speech and my preaching was not with enticing words of man's wisdom, but in demonstration of the Spirit and of power:*

3. In Romans 15:20, Paul talked about building upon another man's foundation, which was Christ's foundation. Paul sought to preach where Christ had not previously been preaching. Here Paul is showing that he is acting according to the Old Testament, which said *that which they had not heard shall they consider* (Isaiah 52:15).

Romans 15:20 *Yea, so have I strived to preach the gospel, not where Christ was named, lest I should build upon another man's foundation:*

Is 52:15 *So shall he sprinkle many nations; the kings shall shut their mouths at him: for that which had not been told them shall they see; and that which they had not heard shall they consider.*

4. In Romans 15:19, Paul talks about the signs and wonders done by the Holy Spirit of God. From Jerusalem and round about Jerusalem Paul fully preached the gospel of Christ.

Romans 15:19 *Through mighty signs and wonders, by the power of the Spirit of God: so that from Jerusalem, and round about unto Jerusalem, I have fully preached the gospel of Christ.*

5. In Romans 15:21 Paul quotes Isaiah 52:15, showing that he has done what the Old Testament said would be done--that the message of Christ would be brought to those that are in ignorance.

Romans 15:21 *But as it is written, To whom he was not spoken of, they shall see: and they that have not heard shall understand.*

Is 52:15 *So shall he sprinkle many nations; the kings shall shut their mouths at him: for that which had not been told them shall they see; and that which they had not heard shall they consider.*

THE POWER AND ASSURANCE OF THE GOSPEL

1. The gospel came not only in words but also in power and in the Holy Ghost, and much assurance.

1 Cor 2:4 *And my speech and my preaching was not with enticing words of man's wisdom, but in demonstration of the Spirit and of power:*

1 Thes 1:5 *For our gospel came not unto you in word only, but also in power, and in the Holy Ghost, and in much assurance; as ye know what manner of men we were among you for your sake.*

2. 1 Corinthians 2:5 tells us our faith should not stand in the wisdom of man, but in the power of God.

1 Cor 2:5 *That your faith should not stand in the wisdom of men, but in the power of God.*

3. 1 Corinthians 2:6 asks the question: *How is it that we speak wisdom among them that are perfect: Yet not the wisdom of this world, nor of the princes of this world, that come to nothing.*

4. Looking again at 1 Corinthians 2:4, Paul mentioned the Spirit is significant. Again the Christians there at Corinth thought they knew a great deal about the Holy spirit. They had experienced various manifestation of the Spirit's power. Yet Paul is talking about the demonstration and power of the Holy Spirit, the Corinthians didn't seem to understand.

WISDOM AND UNDERSTANDING

1. In 1 Corinthians 2:4 Paul denies the use of wisdom; yet he admits to using it, but only among those who are capable of comprehending and appreciating it.

2. Some of the Corinthians couldn't appreciate it because they didn't understand. If you can't comprehend, you can't really appreciate the gospel of Christ since you don't understand it.

3. We can see that 1 Corinthians 2:6 asks the question: How can we speak of the wisdom among them that are perfect? They thought they knew all about the Holy Spirit. Then Paul come along preaching it, denies using wisdom, and yet using it only among those that are capable of comprehending. He did this in verse 4.

1 Cor 2:4 *And my speech and my preaching was not with enticing words of man's wisdom, but in demonstration of the Spirit and of power:*

1 Cor 2:6 *Howbeit we speak wisdom among them that are perfect: yet not the wisdom of this world, nor of the princes of this world, that come to nought:*

4.   In l Corinthians 2:4, Paul said he did not preach with enticing words of man's wisdom. He denies the use of wisdom, but rather demonstrates the spirit and of the power of the Holy Spirit.

5.   Paul admits using wisdom among those who are capable of comprehending and appreciating it. Those who did appreciate it were the perfect ones. There are just some things God is not going to let us know until an appointed time. Paul is teaching that the word of God is in a mystery, even the hidden wisdom which God ordained before the world unto our glory.

1 Cor 2:7   *But we speak the wisdom of God in a mystery, even the hidden wisdom, which God ordained before the world unto our glory.*

6.   Had the princes of this world known, they would not have crucified the Lord Jesus Christ.

1 Cor 2:8 *Which none of the princes of this world knew: for had they known it, they would not have crucified the Lord of glory.*

7.   But as it is written, *Eye hath not seen, nor the ear heard, neither have entered into the heart of man, the things which God hath prepared for them that love him.* (1 Cor 2:9).

ANOINTING OF THE HOLY SPIRIT

Spiritual things are spiritual, they are revealed and taught. 1 John 2:27 says that you do not need to be taught by man, but the holy spirit will teach you all things.

1 Jn 2:27 *But the anointing which ye have received of him abideth in you, and ye need not that any man teach you: but as the same anointing teacheth you of all things, and is truth, and is no lie, and even as it hath taught you, ye shall abide in him.*

2.   The cleansing of lepers and the consecration of the priests required an application of blood. Some literature teaches the way of consecrating is in this order: An application of blood and oil to the right ear, thumb, and big toe of the one cleansed or consecrated. The Bible doesn't say that. According to Leviticus 8:30, Moses consecrated his son and the son's son by sprinkling blood upon them and their garments. That's the law in the Old Testament. In the New Testament, Paul asked Timothy to not neglect the gift that is in him by the laying on of hand and the prophecy. You have two different ways of man coming by the gift of the Holy Spirit.

ANOINTING AND SALVATION

1.   Read 1 John 2:27 again. *The anointing which we have received of him that abideth in us, we need not have any man to teach us but that of the same which is in us.* There is this twofold anointing which stressed the need for salvation, that is the blood of Christ.

2. The need for salvation, the (blood) The anointing of the Holy Spirit (oil) is that the believer might hear the Word of God (ear) to do the works of God (thumb), and walk in the way of God (toe)

3. Illustration: The disciples, who were saved by the blood, were instructed to tarry in Jerusalem until they were given power from on high, and Jesus would send the promise of His Father upon them.

Luke 24:49 *And, behold, I send the promise of my Father upon you: but tarry ye in the city of Jerusalem, until ye be endued with power from on high.*

4. Only then were they able to do the works of God as recorded in Acts.

5. Just as David was anointed with oil, believers need a fresh anointing. Some say you need anointing for each new task we undertake for God. Look at 1 John 2:27, and ask yourself whether you need to be anointed with oil, seeing you have received the Holy Spirit. All we need to be is obedient to the word of God. Jesus Christ has come and fulfilled all of this; God has made that possible. Look what He is saying He will do in Joel.

Joel 2:28 *And it shall come to pass afterward, that I will pour out my spirit upon all flesh; and your sons and your daughters shall prophesy, your old men shall dream dreams, your young men shall see visions.*

BLESSINGS FOR THE FAITHFUL BELIEVER

1. We find similar wording in both the prayer in Isaiah 64:4 and 1 Cor 2:9.

1 Cor 2:9 *But as it is written, Eye hath not seen, nor ear heard, neither have entered into the heart of man, the things which God hath prepared for them that love him.*

Is 64:4 *For since the beginning of the world men have not heard, nor perceived by the ear, neither hath the eye seen, 0 God, beside thee, what he hath prepared for him that waiteth for him.*

2. Psalms 31 talks about how great the goodness, which God has laid up for them that fear Him which trust in Him for the sons of men! Read verses 19 through 24.

Ps 31:19 *Oh how great is thy goodness, which thou hast laid up for them that fear thee; which thou hast wrought for them that trust in thee before the sons of men!*

Ps 31:20 *Thou shalt hide them in the secret of thy presence from the pride of man: thou shalt keep them secretly in a pavilion from the strife of tongues.*

Ps 31:21 *Blessed be the LORD: for he hath shewed me his marvellous kindness in a strong city.*

Ps 31:22 *For I said in my haste, I am cut off from before thine eyes: nevertheless thou heardest the voice of my supplications when I cried unto thee.*

Ps 31:23 *O love the LORD, all ye his saints: for the LORD preserveth the faithful, and plentifully rewardeth the proud doer.*

Ps 31:24 *Be of good courage, and he shall strengthen your heart all ye that hope in the Lord.*

COURAGE AND STRENGTH

1. As believers we are instructed by the expression, I had fainted unless I had believed, (Ps 27:13) to be confident and trust whenever we pray, just as David expresses his complete confidence and trust in God.

2. On this basis we can then feel free to present our petition before God for deliverance or whenever we pray for deliverance from our enemies. Finally we return full circle to trust as the only proper attitude of one who must now wait for God to act.

Ps 27:13 *I had fainted, unless I had believed to see the goodness of the LORD in the land of the living.*

Ps 27:14 *wait on the LORD: be of good courage, and he shall strengthen thine heart: wait, I say, on the LORD.*

3. Isaiah 25:9 shows that this nation waited for the salvation of the Lord. It shows the cities of mankind have fallen into ruin and the nations of the earth have been brought low. Now being humbled before the mighty God who alone has been a refuge from the storm.

Isaiah 25:8 *Yet God will swallow up death in victory, and the Lord God will wipe away all tears.*

1 Cor 15:54 *So when this corruptible shall have put on incorruption, and this mortal shall have put on immortality, then shall be brought to pass the saying that is written, Death is swallowed up in victory.*

Is 25:9 *And it shall be said in that day, Lo, this is our God; we have waited for him, and he will save us: this is the LORD; we have waited for him, we will be glad and rejoice in his salvation.*

FAITH AND WISDOM

1. The gospel which is the wisdom of God, is so powerful that it takes people all the way into heaven. This is past Luke where Jesus said to the woman thy faith have saved you, go in peace.

1 Cor 2:5 *That your faith should not stand in the wisdom of men, but in the power of God.*

Luke 7:50 *And he said to the woman, Thy faith hath saved thee; go in peace.*

2.   In these next few verses, you will be able to see what the Scriptures have been saying when it said eye hath not seen, nor ear heard, neither have entered into the heart of man, the things which God hath prepared for them that love him.

3.   Read Romans 1:2. We see the promise of God previously made by his prophets in the Holy scriptures, concerning his Son Jesus Christ our Lord. Then look at the present time, Romans 6:3-11.

Romans 1:1 *Paul, a servant of Jesus Christ, called to be an apostle, separated unto the gospel of God,*

Romans 1:2 *(Which he had promised afore by his prophets in the holy scriptures,)*

Romans 1:3 *Concerning his Son Jesus Christ our Lord, which was made of the seed of David according to the flesh;*

4.   Romans 6:3-11 bring us into the present.

Romans 6:3 *Know ye not, that so many of us as were baptized into Jesus Christ were baptized into his death?*

Romans 6:4 *Therefore we are buried with him by baptism into death: that like as Christ was raised up from the dead by the glory of the Father, even so we also should walk in newness of life.*

5.   The believer receives daily renewal and treasures of heaven. Here 2-Corinthians is talking about suffering all of the worldly things from the outer man, yet we faint not, the outward man is slowly (dying daily), and yet the inward man is (being renewed daily). Outward is only found here and it is referring to the body, which is in

2 Cor.4:16. Which is corrupted and destroyed. Luke talked about treasures in heaven that faileth not.

2 Cor 4:16 *For which cause we faint not; but though our outward man perish, yet the inward man is renewed day by day.*

Luke 12:33 *Sell that ye have, and give alms; provide yourselves bags which wax not old, a treasure in the heavens that faileth not, where no thief approacheth, neither moth corrupteth.*

James 2:26 *For as the body without the spirit is dead, so faith without works is dead also.*

THE POWER OF GOD

Heb 4:12 *For the word of God is quick, and powerful, and sharper than any two-edged sword, piercing even to the dividing asunder of soul and spirit, and of the joints and marrow, and is a discerner of the thoughts and intents of the heart.*

Romans 1:16 *For I am not ashamed of the gospel of Christ: for it is the power of God unto salvation to everyone that believeth to the Jew first, and also to the Greek.*

PREACHING RIGHTEOUSNESS

Psalms 40:9,10 gives a idea of innocence. Here he said he has preached righteousness in the great congregation: In verse 10, he said I have not hid thy righteousness within his heart, he declared God's faithfulness and thy salvation:

Ps 40:9 I have preached righteousness in the great congregation: 10, I have not refrained my lips, O LORD, thou knowest.

Ps 40:10 *I have not hid thy righteousness within my heart, I have declared thy faithfulness and thy salvation: I have not concealed thy loving kindness and thy truth from the great congregation.*

WISDOM AND THE HOLY SPIRIT

1.   Here in verse 4, Paul mentions the significance of the Spirit. The Corinthians thought they knew a great deal about the Holy Spirit far more than most churches in the apostolic times. They had experienced various manifestation of the Spirit's power.

1 Cor 2:4 *And my speech and my preaching was not with enticing words of (man's wisdom), but in (demonstration) of the (Spirit) and of power:*

2.   Paul denies the use of wisdom; in verse 4, yet he admits to using it, but only to or among those who are capable of comprehending and appreciating it, which are the perfect ones. 1-Corinthians 2:6.

1 Cor 2:6 *Howbeit we speak (wisdom) among them that are (perfect): yet not the (wisdom of this world), nor of the princes of this world, that come to nought:*

1 Cor 2:9 *But as it is written, Eye hath not seen, nor ear heard, neither have entered into the heart of man, the things which God hath prepared for them that love him.*

THE NEW JERUSALEM

1.   Paul insists that God has not forsaken his people Israel.

2.   Isaiah saw a new heaven and a new earth. At this point, Isaiah saw further into the future than any Old Testament prophet, looking beyond the millennial kingdom.

Isaiah 64:4 *For since the beginning of the world men have not heard, nor perceived by the ear, neither hath the eye seen, O God, beside thee, what he hath prepared for him that waiteth for him.*

3.   The New Jerusalem. Weeping and crying shall be no more, God shall wipe away all tears from their eyes, for the former things are passed away.

Rev 21:1 *And I saw a new heaven and a new earth: for the first heaven and the first earth were passed away; and there was no more sea.*

Rev 21:4 *And God shall wipe away all tears from their eyes; and there shall be no more death, neither sorrow, nor crying, neither shall there be any more pain: for the former things are passed away.*

4.   The Old Testament prophet looking beyond the millennial and saw the New Heaven and a New Earth.

Isaiah 65:17 *For, behold, I create new heavens and a new earth: and the former shall not be remembered, nor come into mind.*

Isaiah 65:18 *But be ye glad and rejoice for ever in that which I create: for, behold, I create Jerusalem a rejoicing, and her people a joy.*

Isaiah 65:19 *And I will rejoice in Jerusalem, and joy in my people: and the voice of weeping shall be no more heard in her, nor the voice of crying.*

THE POWER OF THE HOLY SPIRIT

1.   The Corinthians thought they knew a great deal about the Holy Spirit, for more than most churches in the apostolic time. They had experienced various manifestations of the Spirit's power. Paul is saying to them in verse 4, he is not preaching to them enticing word of man's wisdom, but in demonstration of the Spirit's power.

1 Cor 2:4 *And my speech and my preaching was not with enticing words of man's wisdom, but in demonstration of the Spirit and of power:*

2.   In looking at the demonstration of the power of the Holy Spirit. Peter claims to have been one of the eyewitnesses of the transfiguration of Christ, when He was revealed to Peter, James, and John in all of His glory.

3.   There, Jesus was temporarily glorified in the presence of three of His disciples. This was Christ's coming to establish His kingdom. Matthew 17. Yet, we are talking about Paul preaching the power of Jesus Christ. Look how Peter puts it in 2-Peter 1:16.

2 Pet 1:16 *For we have not followed cunningly devised fables, when we made known unto you the power and coming of our Lord Jesus Christ, but were eyewitnesses of his majesty.*

4.   The presence of Moses and Elijah on the mountain represented all those who enter the kingdom by death or the declaration of the Father reinforces Christ's dominion over His kingdom.

APPLICATION OF THE TRANSFIGURATION OF JESUS CHRIST

1.   Since Christians are living expectantly looking forward to the return of Christ, they ought to give Him first place in their lives today, just as He will have in the kingdom.

Matt 17:1 *And after six days Jesus taketh Peter, James, and John his brother, and bringeth them up into an high mountain apart,*

Matt 17:2 *And was transfigured before them: and his face did shine as the sun, and his raiment was white as the light.*

Matt 17:3 *And, behold, there appeared unto them Moses and Elias talking with him.*

Matt 17:4 *Then answered Peter, and said unto Jesus, Lord, it is good for us to be here: if thou wilt, let us make here three tabernacles; one for thee, and one for Moses, and one for Elias.*

Matt 17:5 *While he yet spake, behold, a bright cloud overshadowed them: and behold a voice out of the cloud, which said, This is my beloved Son, in whom I am well pleased; hear ye him.*

Matt 17:6 *And when the disciples heard it, they fell on their face, and were sore afraid.*

Matt 17:7 *And Jesus came and touched them, and said, Arise, and be not afraid.*

Matt 17:8 *And when they had lifted up their eyes, they saw no man, save Jesus only.*

Matt 17:9 *And as they came down from the mountain, Jesus charged them, saying, Tell the vision to no man, until the Son of man be risen again from the dead.*

2.   The power of the coming of our Lord Jesus Christ.

2 Pet 1:16 *For we have not followed cunningly devised fables, when we made known unto you the power and coming of our Lord Jesus Christ, but were eyewitnesses of his majesty.*

Heb 9:12 *Neither by the blood of goats and calves, but by his own blood he entered in once into the holy place, having obtained eternal redemption for us.*

3.   Entering into the Holy Place, the Holy Ghost is significant.   This typopogical picture of the tabernacle, the Holy Spirit was showing that man did not possess direct and complete access to God and could not, while the Old tabernacle with its Mosaic law still stood.

4.   The tabernacle further served as a figure, a physical picture or a symbol, for all to see. Jesus as access was not open to the Holy of Holies, so access to God was not complete. Man's conscience was always left unsatisfied.

5.   Since man must return repeatedly, and since he never knew what happened within the closed chambers, he could never feel he had been completely cleansed.

This would continue only until the time of reformation when Christ would establish a new order, the new covenant. That took place when Christ went into the Holy of Holies. Hebrews 9:11 and 12.

6.   Verse 12 needs to be understood as the Holy of Holies. Look at verse 12, Jesus entered once into the holy place. This takes us back to 1 Corinthians 2:4 and 6. In verse 6 Paul admits to using or preaching wisdom to the perfect ones, those were capable of comprehending and appreciating it. In verse 4 he denies the use of wisdom, by saying his preaching was not with enticing words of man's wisdom, but it demonstrates the Spirit and power:

7.   Mystery refers to some work or purpose of God which was not revealed to us until now. In this case, the reference is to the hidden wisdom, which God ordained unto our glory.

PAUL EXPLAINS THE MYSTERY AND WISDOM OF GOD

1.   The purpose of God concerning our salvation was designed by Him from eternity and is directed toward the everlasting glory that believers will enjoy in His presence. Paul was speaking the wisdom of God in a mystery. This is why the Corinthians didn't understand in verse 6. They were carnal minded.

Romans 16:25 *Now to him that is of power to stablish you according to my gospel, and the preaching of Jesus Christ, according to the revelation of the mystery, which was kept secret since the world began,*

Romans 16:26 *But now is made manifest, and by the scriptures of the prophets, according to the commandment of the everlasting God, made known to all nations for the obedience of faith:*

Romans 16:27 *To God only wise, be glory through Jesus Christ for ever. Amen.*

2.   The unknown is made plain.

Eph 3:3 *How that by revelation he made known unto me the mystery; (as I wrote afore in few words,*

Eph 3:4 *Whereby, when ye read, ye may understand my knowledge in the mystery of Christ)*

Eph 3:5 *Which in other ages was not made known unto the sons of men, as it is now revealed unto his holy apostles and prophets by the Spirit;*

Eph 3:6 *That the Gentiles should be fellow heirs, and of the same body, and partakers of his promise in Christ by the gospel.*

UNIT III:
THE
HOLY
SPIRIT

INTRODUCTION

The third person of the trinity family exercises the power of the Father and Son in creation of redemption. The Holy Spirit of God reveals to Christians the deep things of God and the mystery of Christ (1 Corinthians 2:10-12; Ephesians 3:3-5).

THROUGH THE EYES OF THE HOLY SPIRIT

1. According to the Bible, the third Person of the trinity exercises the power of God the Father and Son in creation and redemption. Because the Holy Spirit is the power through which believers come to Jesus Christ and see with new eyes of faith, He is closer to us than we are to ourselves. Like the eyes of the body through which we see physical things, He is seldom in focus to be seen directly because He is the one through whom all else is seen in a new light. To some extent, this explains why the relationship of the Father and the Son is more prominent in the gospels, because it is through the eyes of the Holy Spirit that the Father-Son relationship is viewed.

2. The Holy Spirit appears in the Gospel of John as the power by which Christians are brought to faith and helped to understand their walk with God. He brings a person to a new birth in Christ by the way of God. Christ said, *No man can come to me except the Father which hath sent me drew him.*

3. That which is born of the flesh is flesh, and that which is born of the Spirit is Spirit. *It is the Spirit who gives life.* The Holy Spirit is the helper, whom Jesus promised to the disciples after His ascension.

4. The triune family of Father, Son, and the Holy Spirit are unified in ministering to believers. It is through the helper that Father and Son abide with the disciples.

5. This unified ministry of the trinity is also as the Spirit brings the world under conviction of sin, righteousness, and judgment. He guides the believers into all truth with what He hears from the Father and the Son.

6. It is a remarkable fact that each one of the Trinitarian family serves the others as all defer to one another: The Son says what He hears from the Father; the Father witnesses to and glorifies the Son; the Father and Son honor the Holy Spirit by commissioning Him to speak in their name; the Holy spirit honors the Father and Son by helping the community of believers.

THE QUALITY OF GENEROSITY

1. The quality of generosity is prominent in the Gospels of Matthew, Mark and Luke where the holy spirit prepares the way for the birth of John the Baptist and Jesus Christ the begotten Son of God.

2.   At the baptism of Jesus, the Spirit of God is present in the form of a dove. This completes the presence of the triune family at the inauguration of the Son's ministry.

3.   Jesus became filled with the Holy Spirit before He was led into the wilderness to be tempted. He was anointed by the Spirit of the Lord in fulfillment of the Old Testament prophecy.

4.   During Christ's ministry, He refers to the Spirit of God as the power by which He is casting out demons, thereby the stronghold of Beelzebub and freeing those held captive.

5.   Accordingly, the Spirit works with the Father and Son in realizing the redeeming power of the kingdom of God. God's kingdom is not only the reign of the Son but also the reign of the spirit, as all share in the reign of the Father.

6.   The Holy Spirit also reveals to Christ the deep things of God and the mystery of Christ. The Holy Spirit acts with God and Christ as the pledge or guarantee by which believers are sealed for the day of salvation, and by which they walk and live and abound in hope with power that is against the lust and the enmity of the flesh.

CHAPTER 12

THE HOLY SPIRIT

Christ through the eternal spirit offered himself without spot unto God. *How much more shall the blood of Christ, who through the eternal Spirit offered himself without spot to God, purge your conscience from dead works to serve the living God?* (Heb. 9:14). Writing about Him, as we do about the person and work of Christ, much of the mystery and misunderstanding as to His work disappear. Let us therefore take up His cross and work in each Dispensation.

THE REVELATION OF GOD

God is a personal Spirit distinct from the world; He is absolutely holy and is invisible to the view of physical, finite as definable limits of sinful minds of mankind.

Although people by themselves can never create truth about God, God has graciously unveiled and manifested Himself to mankind. Other religions and philosophies result from the endless human quest for God; Christianity results from God's quest for lost mankind.

Revelation is God's way of communicating with people concerning Himself, His moral standards, and His plan of salvation. Talking about revelation, Christ chose apostles and trained them to teach the meaning of His death and resurrection, to build the church, and to write the New Testament Scriptures.

We are to remember the words of these eyewitnesses of Christ's resurrection. The content of God's special revelation concerning salvation given to specially gifted spokesmen of the revealed word in Christ is found in *the words which were spoken before by the holy prophets, and of the commandments of the apostles of the Lord and Savior.* The Holy Scriptures are able to provide you knowledge about salvation through faith which is in Christ Jesus.

2 Pet 3:2 *That ye may be mindful of the words which were spoken before by the holy prophets, and of the commandment of us the apostles of the Lord and Savior.*

2 Tim 3:15 *And that from a child thou hast known the holy scriptures, which are able to make thee wise unto salvation through faith which is in Christ Jesus.*

THE GUILT OF MANKIND

God Gave Them up to a Reprobate Mind.

God gave them up. This giving up is not permissive. God lets them do what they want to do.

God withdraws His gracious help. It is judicial—God is the judge, when you don't obey and keep doing the same thing over and over something has to be done.

So God makes a judgment, and that is to leave you over to a reprobate mind, and by doing so, He withdraws His gracious help. It is judicial—God is the administrator of justice or the judge thereof to impose whatever proceedings therein as the judicial power proceedings are.

God enforced the judicial power just as the courts would. You could say it is related to judgment--as a judicial mind which belongs to a judge. Leaving one over to a reprobate mind is a judgment of God who made the divine judgment.

They are blinded not because God withdraws His light, but because of the judicial act of God whereby He delivered them over to the natural result of their unbelief and action. When they followed the lie they began to walk in, it is the way of conforming to the lie and results in a lifestyle in opposition to God.

The Life-style of the Reprobate Mind

Three results of the Gentiles' rejection are given. God give them up to all forms of uncleanness and its consequent actions (Romans 1:24-25).

Eph 4:18-19 *Having the understanding darkened, being alienated from the life of God through the ignorance that is in them, because of the blindness of their heart. [19] Who being past feeling have given themselves over unto lasciviousness, to work all uncleanness with greediness.*

1 Cor 6:18 *Flee fornication. Every sin that a man doeth is without the body; but he that committeth fornication sinneth against his own body.*

Lev 18:22 *Thou shalt not lie with mankind, as with womankind: it is abomination.*

THE WORK OF THE HOLY SPIRIT IN CREATION

1. *He has garnished the heavens.* He made them beautiful with stars and sun. The work of the Trinity in creation has been described as God the Father, the creator, God the Son molded it into shape, as it is seen in the heavens, and every visible object, God the Holy Spirit breathed into all creation of life. This is confirmed by the account of the creation of man in Genesis 2:7. One reference to the work of the holy spirit in creation is Job 26:13, *By his spirit he hath garnished the heavens; his hand hath formed the crooked serpent.*

2.   We read in Gen 2:7, *And the LORD God formed man of the dust of the ground, and breathed into his nostrils the breath of life; and man became a living soul.*   Man became a living soul.   Here we can see the threefold work of God. The Father made the dust of the ground, the Son, like a sculptor molds the clay into a statue, formed the dust into the shape of a man, and the Holy Spirit breathed into its nostrils the *breath of life.*

3.   *The Holy Spirit moved upon the face of the water.* Gen 1:2 *And the earth was without form, and void; and darkness was upon the face of the deep. And the Spirit of God moved upon the face of the waters.*

THE HOLY SPIRIT DRAWS US

1.   The third person of the trinity exercises the power of the Father and the Son in creation and redemption. Because the Holy Spirit is the power by which believers come to Christ and see with new eyes of faith.

2.   When we read John 6:44 we must consider the power of the Holy Spirit. There it tells us *no man can come to Christ except the Father draw him.* The Holy Spirit is closer to us than we are to ourselves. Like the eyes of the body through which we see physical things, He is seldom in focus to be seen directly.

3.   In John 6:44 Jesus says, *No man can come to me, except the Father which hath sent me draw him; and I will raise him up at the last day.* This explains why the relationship of the Father and the Son is more prominent in the gospels, because it is through the eyes of the Holy Spirit that the Father Son relationship is viewed.

4.   As we can see the Holy Spirit appears in the gospel of John as the power by which Christians are brought to a new birth. It gives life. The Scripture says, *That which is born of the flesh is flesh; and that which is born of the Spirit is spirit (John 3:6).*   John also says, *It is the spirit that quickeneth; the flesh profiteth nothing; the words, that I speak unto you, they are spirit, and they are life (John 6:63).*

THE PROMISE OF A COMFORTER

1.   John 14:16 *And I will pray the Father, and he shall give you another Comforter, that he may abide with you forever.*

2.   Jesus promises in John 14:26, *But the Comforter, which is the Holy Ghost, whom the Father will send in my name, he shall teach you all things, and bring all things to your remembrance, whatsoever I have said unto you.*   It is through the Helper that the Father and Son abide with the disciples.

3.   In John 15:26 Jesus again says, *But when the Comforter is come, whom I will send unto you from the Father, even the Spirit of truth, which proceedeth from the Father, he shall testify of me.*

CHAPTER 13

REDEMPTION

Redemption means deliverance by a payment of a price. According to the New Testament, redemption refers to salvation from sin, death, and the wrath of God by Christ's sacrifice. According to Old Testament scripture, redemption was applied to property, animals, persons, and the nation of Israel as a whole--In most instances, freedom from obligation, bondage, or danger was secured by the payment of a price.

NEW TESTAMENT MEANING OF REDEMPTION

1. In the New Testament, redemption is referred to as loosing and loosing away. Luke describes *a widow of about fourscore and four years, which departed not from the temple, but yet served God with fasting and prayers…and she coming in that instant gave thanks likewise unto the Lord, and spake of him to all them that looked for redemption in Jerusalem* (Luke 2:37-38).

2. Romans 3:24 talks about *Being justified freely by His grace through the redemption that is in Christ Jesus.*

3. Hebrews 9:12 explains that no blood of goats and calves was shed for Jesus; rather, by his own blood Jesus entered into the Holy place, having obtained eternal redemption for us.

4. Again we find Luke talking about redemption in another way which had another meaning. This time he talks about seeing *the Son of man coming in a cloud with power and great glory. And when these things begin to come to pass, then look up and lift up your heads; for your redemption draweth nigh* (Luke 21:27-28).

5. Ephesians 4:30 talks about being sealed until the day of redemption. Having been sealed by the Holy Spirit will take us back to the gospel of John where Jesus says, *No man can come to me, except the Father which hath sent me draw him; and I will raise him up at the last day* (John 6:44).

Now we can understand the meaning of the sayings which is the earnest of our inheritance until the redemption of the purchased possession unto the praise of his glory. Having that glory seal of promise that God has given to all who believe and accept the word of truth through our Lord and savior Jesus Christ. I truly hope we have a better understanding about redemption and the Holy Spirit. This is just like God is sitting and talking with you in person because it is His word.

OLD TESTAMENT: REDEMPTION BY PAYMENT OF MONEY

1. In Leviticus, the word redemption refers to redemption by a kinsman. Lev 25:24 *And in all the land of your possession ye shall grant a redemption for the land.*

Lev 25:51-52 If *there be yet* many years *behind*, according unto them he shall give again the price of his redemption out of the money that he was bought for. And if there remain but few years unto the year of jubile, then he shall count with him, *and* according unto his years shall he give him again the price of his redemption.

2. In Numbers 3:48-51 redemption means money. Here we find them talking about giving the money *And Moses gave the money of them that were redeemed, unto Aaron and his sons.*

Num 3:48-51 *And thou shalt give the money, wherewith the odd number of them is to be redeemed, unto Aaron and· to his sons. [49] And Moses took the redemption money of them that were over and above them that were redeemed by the Levites: [50] Of the firstborn of the children of Israel took he the money; a thousand three hundred and threescore and five shekels, after the shekel of the sanctuary: [51] And Moses gave the money of them that were redeemed unto Aaron and to his sons, according to the word of the LORD, as the LORD commanded Moses.*

REDEMPTION AS LOOSING and LOOSING AWAY

1. Luke 2:38 *And she coming in that instant gave thanks likewise unto the Lord, and spake of him to all them that looked for redemption in Jerusalem.*

2. Heb 9:12 *Neither by the blood of goats and calves, but by his own blood-he entered in once into the holy place, having obtained eternal redemption for us.*

3. Luke 21:26-28 *Men's hearts failing them for fear, and for looking after those things which are coming on the earth: for the powers of heaven shall be shaken. [27] And then shall they see the Son of man coming in a cloud with power and great glory. [28] And when these things begin to come to pass, then look up, and lift up your heads; for your redemption draweth nigh.*

BEING JUSTIFIED THROUGH REDEMPTION BY FAITH

Romans 3:24-26 *Being justified freely by his grace through the redemption that is in Christ Jesus: [25] Whom God hath set forth to be a propitiation through faith in his blood, to declare his righteousness for the remission of sins that are past, through the forbearance of God. [26] To declare, I say, at this time his righteousness: that he might be just, and the justifier of him which believeth in Jesus.*

HEARING THE WORD OF TRUTH

Eph 1:13-14 *In whom ye also trusted, after that ye heard the word of truth, the gospel of your salvation: in whom also after that ye believed, ye were sealed with that holy Spirit of promise, [14] Which is the earnest of our inheritance until the redemption of the purchased possession, unto the praise of his glory.*

According to Old Testament scripture, redemption was applied to property, animals, persons, and the nation of Israel as a whole. In most instances, freedom from obligation, bondage, or danger was secured by the payment of a price.

OLD TESTAMENT REDEMPTION

A ransom bribe, satisfaction, or sum of money paid to obtain freedom, favor, or reconciliation. Man may redeem property, animals, and individuals (slaves, prisoners), but God alone, is able to redeem mankind from the slavery of sin.

Ps 130:7-8 *Let Israel hope in the LORD: for with the LORD there is mercy, and with him is plenteous redemption. [8] And he shall redeem Israel from all his iniquities.*

Deut 15:15 *And thou shalt remember that thou wast a bondman in the land of Egypt, and the LORD thy God redeemed thee: therefore I command thee this thing today.*

THE POWER OF DEATH THROUGH THE REDEEMER

Job 19:25-29 *For I know that my redeemer liveth, and that he shall stand at the latter day upon the earth: [26] And though after my skin worms destroy this body, yet in my flesh shall I see God: [27] Whom I shall see for myself, and mine eyes shall behold, and not another; though my reins be consumed within me. [28] But ye should say, Why persecute we him, seeing the root of the matter is found in me? [29] Be ye afraid of the sword: for wrath bringeth the punishments of the sword, that ye may know there is a judgment.*

Psalms 49:8-9 *For the redemption of their soul is precious, and it ceaseth for ever: [9] That he should still live for ever, and not see corruption.*

COST OF REDEMPTION: THE BLOOD OF CHRIST

The New Testament emphasizes the cost of redemption--the precious blood of Christ which is called an atoning sacrifice.

1. Peter emphasized the precious blood of Christ as of a lamb without blemish and without spot. *Who verily was foreordained before the foundation of the world, and was manifest in these last times for you* (1 Pet 1:20).

2.   *Who by him do believe in God, that raised him from the dead, and gave him glory: that your faith and hope might be in God* (1 Pet 1:21).

3.   Ephesians explains about the redemption through Christ's blood, the forgiveness of sin, according to the riches of his grace. *That the God of our Lord Jesus Christ, the Father of glory, may give unto you the spirit of wisdom and revelation in the knowledge of him: The eyes of your understanding being enlightened: that ye may know what is the hope of his calling, and what the riches of the glory of his inheritance in the saints* (Eph 1:17-18).

4.   By his blood, Jesus is the atoning sacrifice. *Whom God hath set forth to be a propitiation through faith in his blood, to declare his righteousness for the remission of sins that are past, through the forbearance of God* (Romans 3:25).

5.   1 Corinthians explains redemption as a motivation to personal holiness in saying, what with a question? *Know you not that your body is the temple of the Holy Ghost which is in you, for you are bought with a price?* (1 Cor 6:19-20)

6.   I like the way Peter puts it. He says, *Wherefore gird up the loins of your mind, be sober, and hope to the end for the grace that is to be brought unto you at the revelation of Christ Jesus* (1 Pet 1:13).

7.   Look at 1 Pet 1:14. Don't you just love it. *As obedient children, not fashioning yourselves according to the former lusts in your ignorance.* Look how he puts it. *In your ignorance*, as if you don't know any better.

8.   Peter went on to say, *as he which hath called you is holy, so you be holy in all manner of conversation; because it is written you are to be holy because He is Holy. If God the Father who without respect of persons judgeth according to every man's work.* (1 Pet 1:15-17)

9.   *Forasmuch as you know that you were not redeemed with corruptible things, but with the precious blood of Christ, not as silver and gold.* (1 Pet 1:18)

ATONING SACRIFICE BY HIS BLOOD

Romans 3:25 *Whom God hath set forth to be a propitiation through faith in his blood, to declare his righteousness for the remission of sins that are past, through the forbearance of God.*

REDEMPTION AS A MOTIVATION TO PERSONAL HOLINESS

1 Cor 6:19-20 *What? Know ye not that your body is the temple of the Holy Ghost which is in you, which ye have of God, and ye are not your own? [20] For ye are bought with a price: therefore glorify God in your body, and in your spirit, which are God's.*

1 Pet 1:13-19 *Wherefore gird up the loins of your mind, be sober, and hope to the end for the grace that is to be brought unto you at the revelation of Jesus Christ. [14] As obedient children, not fashioning*

yourselves according to the former lust in your ignorance. [15] But as he which hath called you is holy, so be ye holy in all manner of conversation. [16] Because it is written, Be ye holy; for I am holy. [17] And if ye call on the Father, who without respect of persons judgeth according to every man's work, pass the time of your sojourning here in fear. [18] Forasmuch as ye know that ye were not redeemed with corruptible things, as silver and gold, from your vain conversation received by tradition from your fathers. [19] But with the precious blood of Christ, as of a lamb without blemish and without spot.

THE SLAVERY OF SIN

According to the Bible, the writers also emphasize the result of redemption: in freedom from sin and freedom to serve God through Jesus Christ our Lord.

John 8: 34 *Jesus answered them, Verily, verily, I say unto you, Whosoever committeth sin is the servant of sin.*

Romans 6:18 *Being then made free from sin, ye became the servants of righteousness.*

FREE FROM SIN AND THE LAW

How can we fail to rejoice, having been made free from the bondage of slavery to sin.

Gal 4:3-5 *Even so we, when we were children, were in bondage under the elements of the world: [4] But when the fullness of the time was come, .God sent forth his Son, made of a woman, made under the law, [5] To redeem them that were under the law, that we might receive the adoption of sons.*

Gal 5:1 *Stand fast therefore in the liberty wherewith Christ hath made us free, and be not entangled again with the yoke of bondage.*

THE FEAR OF DEATH

Heb 2:14-15 *Forasmuch then as the children are partakers of flesh and 'blood', he also himself, likewise took part of ,the same; that through death he might destroy him that had the power of death, that is, the devil; [15] And deliver them who through fear of death were all: their lifetime subject to bondage.*

THE SON SHALL MAKE YOU FREE

John 8:36 *If the Son therefore shall make you free, ye shall be free indeed.*

THE UNIFIED MINISTRY

This unified ministry of the trinity is also seen as the spirit brings the world under conviction of sin, righteousness, and judgment. He guides the believers into all truth with what He hears from the Father and the Son.

John 15:26 *But when the Comforter is come, whom I will send unto you from the Father, even the Spirit of truth, which proceedeth from the Father, he shall testify of me:*

THE SON HEARS FROM THE FATHER

For I have not spoken of myself; but the Father which sent me, he gave me a commandment, what I should say, and what I should speak. And, I know that his commandment is life everlasting: whatsoever I speak therefore, even as the Father said unto me, so I speak (John 12:49-50).

THE FATHER WITNESSES AND GLORIFIES THE SON

John 8:16-18 *And yet if I judge, my judgment is true: for I am not alone, but I and the Father that sent me. [17] It is also written in your law, that the testimony of two men is true. [18] I am one that bears witness of myself, and the Father that sent me beareth witness of me.*

John 8:50 *And I seek not mine own glory: there is one that seeketh and judgeth.*

John 8:54 *Jesus answered. If I honour myself, my honour is nothing: it is my Father that honoureth me of whom ye say, that he is your God.'*

THE FATHER AND SON COMMISSION THE HOLY SPIRIT

John 14:16 *And I will pray the Father, and he shall give you another Comforter, that he may abide with you for ever.*

John 14:26 *But the Comforter, which is the Holy Ghost, whom the Father will send in my name, he shall teach you all things, and bring all things to your remembrance, whatsoever I have said unto you.*

1. The Father and Son honor the Holy Spirit by commissioning Him to speak in their name as we read in John 14 verses 16 and 26. The Holy Spirit honors the Father and Son by helping the community of believers.

2. According to the Bible, like Father and Son, the Holy spirit is at the disposal of the other persons of the trinity family, and all three are one in being at the disposal of the redeemed family of the believers.

3. The Holy Spirit's attitude and ministry according to the Bible are marked by generosity. His chief function is to light up Jesus' teaching, to glorify His person, and to work in the life of the individual believers and the church who are the believers in Christ Jesus' teaching.

QUALITY OF GENEROSITY

1.   So again, according to the Bible, the quality of the generosity is prominent in the Gospels of Matthew, Mark, and Luke. The Holy Spirit prepares the way for the births of John the Baptist and Jesus Christ the Son.

2.   At the baptism of Jesus, the Spirit of God is present in the form of a dove. This completes the presence of the triune family at the inauguration of the Son's ministry. Matthew 3:16-17; Mark 1:9-11; Luke 3:21-22; John 1:33.

The Quality of Generosity Prominent in the Gospels

First let us look at the quality of the generosity that is prominent in the Gospels of Matthew and Luke.

Matt 1:20 *But while he thought on these things, behold, the angel of the Lord appeared unto him in a dream, saying, Joseph, thou son of David, fear not to take unto thee Mary thy wife: for that which is conceived in her is of the Holy Ghost.*

Luke 1:15 *For he shall be great in the sight of the Lord, and shall drink neither wine nor strong drink; and he shall be filled with the Holy Ghost, even from his mother's womb.*

Luke 1:35 *And the angel answered and said unto her, The Holy Ghost shall come upon thee, and the power of the Highest shall overshadow thee: therefore also that holy thing which shall be born of thee shall be called the Son of God.*

Luke 1:41 *And it came to pass, that, when Elisabeth heard the salutation of Mary, the babe leaped in her womb; and Elisabeth was filled with the Holy Ghost.*

CHAPTER 14

THE MINISTRY OF JESUS CHRIST

Let us look at the references in each of the Gospels of the Baptism of Jesus at the completion of the presence of the triune family with the dove as the Spirit of God being present.

Matt 3:16-17 *And Jesus, when he was baptized, went up straightway out of the water: and, lo, the heavens were opened unto him, and he saw the Spirit of God descending like a dove, and lighting upon him: [17] And lo a voice from heaven, saying, This is my beloved Son, in whom I am well pleased.*

Mark 1:9-11 *And it came to pass in those days, that Jesus came from Nazareth of Galilee, and was baptized of John in Jordan. [10] And straightway coming up out of the water, he saw the heavens opened, and the Spirit like a dove descending upon him: [11] And there came a voice from heaven, saying, Thou art my beloved Son, in whom I am well pleased.*

Luke 3:21-22 *Now when all the people were baptized, it came to pass, that Jesus also being baptized, and praying, the heaven was opened, [22] And the Holy Ghost descended in a bodily shape like a dove upon him, and a voice came from heaven, which said, Thou art my beloved Son; in thee I am well pleased.*

John 1:33 *And I knew him not: but he that sent me to baptize with water, the same said unto me, Upon whom thou shalt see the Spirit descending, and remaining on him, the same is he which baptizeth with the Holy Ghost.*

FULFILLMENT OF THE OLD TESTAMENT PROPHECY

According to the Bible, Jesus is also filled with the Holy Spirit as He is led into the wilderness to be tempted. It is said He is anointed by the Spirit of the Lord in fulfillment of the Old Testament prophecy.

Isaiah 61:1 *The spirit of the Lord GOD is upon me; because the LORD hath anointed me to preach good tidings unto the meek; he hath sent me to bind up the brokenhearted, to proclaim liberty to the captives, and the opening of the prison to them that are bound.*

JESUS REFERS TO THE SPIRIT OF GOD

1.   According to Matthew and Luke, during Jesus' ministry Jesus refers to the spirit of God, as the power by which He is casting out demons, thereby the stronghold of Beelzebul and freeing those held captive.

2.   Accordingly, the spirit works with the Father and Son in realizing the redeeming power of the kingdom of God. God's kingdom is not only the reign of the Son but also the reign of the Spirit, as they all share ·in the· reign of the Father.

Matt 12:28-29 *But if I cast out devils by the Spirit of God, then the kingdom of God is come unto you. [29] Or else how can one enter into a strong man's house, and spoil his goods, except he first bind the strong man? and then he will spoil his house.*

Luke 11:20 *But if I with the finger of God cast out devils, no doubt the kingdom of God is come upon you.*

3.   The person and the ministry of the Holy Spirit in the Gospels is confirmed by His work in the early church.

BAPTISM BY THE HOLY SPIRIT

The baptism by the Holy Spirit is the pouring out of the Spirit's power in missions evangelism. This prophecy of Jesus begins on Pentecost.

Acts 1:5 For John truly baptized with water; but ye shall be baptized with the Holy Ghost not many days hence.

POWER BY THE HOLY SPIRIT

Acts 1:8 But ye shall receive power, after that the Holy Ghost is come upon you; and ye shall be witnesses unto me both in Jerusalem, and in all Judaea, and in Samaria, and unto the uttermost part of the earth.

PROPHECY OF THE SPIRIT UPON ALL FLESH

Joel 2:28-32 *And it shall come to pass afterward, that I will pour out my spirit upon all flesh; and your sons and your daughters shall prophesy, your old men shall dream dreams, your young men shall see visions: [29] And also upon the servants and upon the handmaids in those days will I pour out my spirit. [30] And I will shew wonders in the heavens and in the earth, blood, and fire, and pillars of smoke. [31] The sun shall be turned into darkness, and the moon into blood, before the great and the terrible day of the LORD come. [32] And it shall come to pass, that whosoever shall call on the name of the LORD shall be delivered: for in mount Zion and in Jerusalem shall be deliverance, as the LORD hath said, and in the remnant whom the LORD shall call.*

THE PROPHECY OF JESUS BEGINS ON PENTECOST

Many of those who hear of the finished work of God in Jesus' death and resurrection repent of their sins. In this act of repentance, they receive the gift of the Holy Spirit and become witnesses of God's grace through the Holy Spirit.

Acts 2:1-3 *And when the day of Pentecost was fully come, they were all with one accord in one place. [2] And suddenly there came a sound from heaven as of a rushing mighty wind, and it filled all the house where they were sitting. [3] And there appeared unto them cloven tongues like as of fire, and it sat upon each of them.*

THE FINISHED WORK IN CHRIST JESUS

Acts 2:32 *This Jesus hath God raised up, whereof we all are witnesses.*

THE PROMISE OF THE GIFT OF THE HOLY SPIRIT

Acts 2:33-38 *Therefore being by the right hand of God exalted, and having received of the Father the promise of the Holy Ghost, he hath shed forth this, which ye now see and hear. [34] For David is not ascended into the heavens: but he saith himself, The LORD said unto my Lord, Sit thou on my right hand, [35] Until I make thy foes thy footstool. [36] Therefore let all the house of Israel· know assuredly, that God hath made that same Jesus, whom ye have crucified, both Lord and Christ. [37] Now when they heard this, they were pricked in their heart, and said unto Peter and to the rest of the apostles, Men and brethren, what shall we do? [38] Then Peter said unto them, Repent, and be baptized every one of you in the name of Jesus Christ for the remission of sins, and ye shall receive the gift of the Holy Ghost.*

Acts 2:38-39 *Then Peter said unto them, Repent, and be baptized every one of you in the name of Jesus Christ for the remission of sins, and ye shall receive the gift of the Holy Ghost. [39] For the promise is unto you, and to your children, and to all that are afar off, even as many as the Lord our God shall call.*

JESUS CHRIST IS LORD

1.   From Bible scripture we learn that Paul's teaching about the Holy Spirit harmonizes with the accounts of the Spirit's activity in the Gospels and Acts. According to Paul, it is by the Holy Spirit that confesses that Jesus is Lord.

2.   Through the same Spirit gifts are given to the body of Christ to ensure it richness and unity. The Holy Spirit is the way to Jesus Christ the Son and to the Father. He is the person who bears witness to us that we are the children of God. He makes intercession for us with groaning which cannot be uttered.

1 Cor 12:3 *Wherefore I give you to understand, that no man speaking by the Spirit of God calleth Jesus accursed: and that no man can say that Jesus is the Lord, but by the Holy Ghost.*

GIFTS OF THE SPIRIT

1 Cor 12:4-12 *Now there are diversities of gifts, but the same spirit. [5] And there are differences of administrations, but the same Lord. [6] And there are diversities of operations, but it is the same God which worketh all in all. [7] But the manifestation of the Spirit is given to every man to profit withal. [8] For to one is given by the Spirit the word of wisdom; to another the word of knowledge by the same Spirit; [9] To another faith by the same Spirit; to another the gifts of healing by the same Spirit; [10] To another the working of miracles; to another prophecy; to another discerning of spirits; to another divers kinds of tongues; to another the interpretation of tongues: [11] But all these worketh that one and the selfsame Spirit, dividing to every man severally as he will. [12] For as the body is one, and hath many members, and all the members of that one body, being many, are one body: so also is Christ.*

The Way to Jesus Christ

Romans 8: 11 *But if the Spirit of him that raised up Jesus from the dead dwell in you, he that raised up Christ from the dead shall also quicken your mortal bodies by his Spirit that dwelleth in you.*

Romans 8:14-15 *For as many as are led by the Spirit of God, they are the sons of God. [15] For ye have not received the spirit of bondage again to fear; but ye have received the Spirit of adoption, whereby we cry, Abba, Father.*

The Spirit Bears Witness that We are Children of God

Romans 8:16-17 *The Spirit itself beareth witness with our spirit, that we are the children of God: [17] And if children, then heirs; heirs of, God, and joint-heirs with Christ; if so be that we suffer with him, that we may be also glorified together.*

The Holy Spirit Makes Intercession

Romans 8:26-27 *Likewise the Spirit also helpeth our infirmities: for we know not what we should pray for as we ought: but the Spirit itself maketh intercession for us with groanings which cannot be uttered. [27] And he that searcheth the hearts knoweth what is the mind of the Spirit, because he maketh intercession for the saints according to the will of God.*

The Holy Spirit Reveals the Deep Things of God

1. The Holy Spirit reveals to the Christians the deep things of God according to the Bible, and the mystery of Christ. The Holy Spirit acts with God and Christ as the pledge or guarantee by which believers are sealed for the day of salvation.

2.   The Holy Spirit walks and lives in the believer in Christ, and abounds in power against the lust and enmity of the flesh. Paul contrasts the fruit of the Spirit according to the Bible.

1 Cor 2:10-12 *But God hath revealed them unto us by his Spirit: for the Spirit searcheth all things, yea, the deep things of God. [11] For what man knoweth the things of a man, save the spirit of man which is in him? even so the things of God knoweth no man, but the Spirit of God. [12] Now we have received, not the spirit of the world, but the spirit which is of God; that we might know the things that are freely given to us of God.*

The Holy Spirit Reveals the Mystery of Jesus Christ

Eph 3:3-5 *How that by revelation he made known unto me the mystery; (as I wrote afore in few words, [4] Whereby, when ye read, ye may understand my knowledge in the mystery of Christ)*

[5] Which in other ages was not made known unto the sons of men, as it is now revealed unto his holy apostles and prophets by the Spirit.

The Holy Spirit which Stablisheth

2 Cor 1:21-22 *Now he which stablisheth us with you in Christ, and hath anointed us, is God; [22] Who hath also sealed us, and given the earnest of the Spirit in our hearts.*

The Holy Spirit Walks and Lives in the Believers

Romans 15:13 *Now the God of hope fills you with all joy and peace in believing, that ye may abound in hope, through the power of the Holy Ghost.*

Contrasts of the Fruit of the Holy Spirit

Gal 5:22-23 *But the fruit of the Spirit is love, joy, peace, longsuffering, gentleness, goodness, faith, [23] Meekness, temperance: against such there is no law.*

Sealed Unto the Day of Redemption

Since the Holy Spirit is the expressed power of the triune family, it is that no one is to grieve the Holy Spirit of God. Since there is no further appeal to the Father and Son on the day of redemption is available.

Eph 4:30 *And grieve not the Holy Spirit of God, whereby ye are sealed unto the day of redemption.*

Christian Liberty Stems from the Work of the Holy Spirit

1. It is said that Christian liberty stems from the work of the Holy Spirit: where the spirit of the Lord is, there is liberty according to the Bible. This is a process of beholding as in a mirror the glory of the Lord, and being transformed into the same image from glory to glory.

2. Just as by the Spirit of the Lord, the personal work of the Holy Spirit is according to one with that of the Father and Son. The grace of the Lord Jesus Christ, and the love of God, and the sweet communion of the Holy Spirit be with you all. AMEN.

2 Cor 3:17-18 *Now the Lord is that Spirit: and where the Spirit of the Lord is, there is liberty. [18] But we all, with open face: beholding as in a glass the glory of the Lord, are changed into the same image from glory to glory, even as by the Spirit of the Lord.*

Sweet Communion of the Holy Spirit

2 Cor 13:14 *The grace of the Lord Jesus Christ, and the love of God, and the communion of the Holy Ghost, be with you all. Amen.*

THE PROFOUND TEACHINGS OF GOD AND JESUS CHRIST

1. Among the New Testament writings the Spirit's ministry is evident in the profound teaching which shows the relationship of God, and Christ, and the eternal Spirit.

2. The Holy Spirit's work in the Old Testament shows the coming of Christ is explained in this and other passages in the Bible.

Heb 9:14 *How much more shall the blood of Christ, who through the eternal spirit offered himself without spot to God, purge your conscience from dead works to serve the living God?*

The Relationship of God, Christ, and the Eternal Spirit

The Holy Spirit's work is explained in this and the preparation for the coming of Christ which is from the Old Testament passages in the New Testament.

Heb 3:7 *Wherefore (as the Holy Ghost saith, Today if ye will hear his voice.*

Heb 9:8 *The Holy Ghost this signifying, that the way into the holiest of all was not yet made manifest, while as the first tabernacle was yet standing.*

Heb 10:15-17 *Whereof the Holy Ghost also is a witness to us: for after that he had said before, [16] This is the covenant that I will make with them after those days, SAITH THE Lord, I will put my laws into their hearts, and in their minds will I write them: [17] And their sins and iniquities will I remember no more.*

THE WORK OF THE SPIRIT IN THE OLD TESTAMENT

1. To consider the working of the spirit in the Old Testament in light of Christ's ministry in the New Testament. The Spirit is the energy of God in creation. God endows man with personal life by breathing into his nostrils the breath of life.

2. The Spirit strives with fallen men and comes upon certain judges and warriors with charismatic power. The spirit departed from Saul, because of his disobedience.

The Energy of God in Creation

Gen 1:2 *And the earth was without form, and void; and darkness was upon the face of the deep. And the Spirit of God moved upon the face of the waters.*

Job 26:13 *By his spirit he hath garnished the heavens; his hand hath formed the crooked serpent.*

Isaiah 32:15 *Until the spirit be poured upon us from on high, and the wilderness be a fruitful field, and the fruitful field be counted for a forest.*

The Personal Endowed Spirit of God in Man

Gen 2:7 *And the LORD God formed man of the dust of the ground, and breathed into his nostrils the breath of life; and man became a living soul.*

The Spirit Strives with Fallen Man

Gen 6:3 *And the LORD said, My spirit shall not always strive with man, for that he also is flesh: yet his days shall be an hundred and twenty years.*

A Judge with Charismatic Power

Judges 14:6 *And the Spirit of the LORD came mightily upon him, and he rent him as he would have rent a kid, and he had nothing in his hand: but he told not his father or his mother what he had done.*

Old Testament Prophecy

1. In the long span of the Old Testament prophecy, Scripture tells that the Spirit plays a prominent role. David declared, *The Spirit of the Lord spoke by me, And His word was on my tongue* (2 Sam 23:2). Ezekiel claimed that the Spirit entered him when he spoke to him (Ezek 2:2).

2. The Spirit also inspired holiness in the Old Testament believers. It also promised to give a new heart to God's people. God said, *I will put my Spirit within you, and cause you to walk in my statutes* (Ezek 36:27).

2 Sam 23:2 *The spirit of the LORD spake by me, and his word was in my tongue.*

Ezek 2:2 *And the spirit entered into me when he spake unto me, and set me upon my feet, that I heard him that spake unto me.*

Psalms 143:10 *Teach me to do thy will; for thou art my God: thy spirit is good; lead me into the land of uprightness.*

Ezek 36:27 *And I will put my spirit within you, and cause you to walk in my statutes, and ye shall keep my judgments, and do them.*

The Word of the Spirit in the Ministry of the Messiah

1. The work of the ministry of the Messiah in the prophecy of Isaiah is a preview of the work of the Father, the spirit, and Son, who is the branch of Jesse.

2. Looking forward to the ministry of Jesus Christ, the Holy Spirit inspired Isaiah to prophecy: *The spirit of the Lord shall rest Upon Him* (Isaiah 11:1-5; 11:2).

ISAIAH 11:1-5 *A shoot shall come out from the stump of Jesse, and a branch shall grow out of his roots. [2] The spirit of the LORD shall rest on him, the spirit of wisdom and understanding, the spirit of counsel and might, the spirit of knowledge and the fear of the LORD. [3] His delight shall be in the fear of the LORD. He shall not judge by what his eyes see, or decide by what his ears hear; [4] but with righteousness he shall judge the poor, and decide with equity for the meek of the earth; he shall strike the earth with the rod of his mouth, and with the breath of his lips he shall kill the wicked. [5] Righteousness shall be the belt around his waist, and faithfulness the belt around his loins.*

The Holy Spirit Inspired and Fulfilled Prophecy

1. Jesus Christ was inspired by the Holy Spirit with wisdom, understanding, counsel, might, knowledge, fear of the Lord, righteousness, and faithfulness.

2. Here we come to the full cycle of the New Testament where Jesus is claiming the fulfillment of this prophecy in Himself. Isaiah 42:1 summarized the redeeming work of the Father, Son, and spirit in the salvation of the lost, as God spoke through the prophet: *Behold! My Servant whom I uphold; My Elect, in whom my soul delights! I have put my Spirit upon Him: He will bring forth justice to the Gentiles.*

3. There isn't any clearer reflection of the intimate interworking of the triune family and the Spirit's powerful role that can be found in the Old Testament than in this prophecy. It ties God's grace in the Old and New Testament together in remarkable harmony.

Isaiah 61:1-2 *The Spirit of the Lord GOD is upon me: because the LORD hath anointed me to preach good tidings unto the meek; he hath sent me to bind up the brokenhearted, to proclaim liberty to the captives, and the opening of the prison to them that are bound; [2] To proclaim the acceptable year of the LORD, and the day of vengeance of our God; to comfort all that mourn.*

Luke 4:18-19 *The Spirit of the Lord is upon me, because he hath anointed me to preach the gospel to the poor; he hath sent me to heal the brokenhearted, to preach deliverance to the captives, and recovering of sight to the blind, to set at liberty them that are bruised, [19] To preach the acceptable year of the Lord.*

Salvation in the Lost

Isaiah 42:1-4 *Behold my servant, whom I uphold; mine elect, in whom my soul delighteth; I have put my spirit upon him: he shall bring forth judgment to the Gentiles.[2] He shall not cry, nor lift up, nor cause his voice to be heard in the street. [3]A bruised reed shall he not break, and the smoking flax shall he not quench: he shall bring forth judgment unto truth. [4] He shall not fail nor be discouraged, till he have set judgment in the earth: and the isles shall wait for his law.*

Isaiah 42:5-9 *Thus saith God the LORD, he that created the heavens, and stretched them out; he that spread forth the earth, and that which cometh out of it; he that giveth breath unto the people upon it, and spirit to them that walk therein: [6] I the LORD have called thee in righteousness, and will hold thine hand, and will keep thee, and give thee for a covenant of the people, for a light of the Gentiles; [7] To open the blind eyes, to bring out the prisoners from the prison, and them that sit in darkness out of the prison house. [8] I am the LORD: that is my name: and my glory will I not give to another, neither my praise to graven images. [9] Behold, the former things are come to pass, and new things do I declare: before they spring forth I tell you of them.*

Christ Brings Justice to the Gentiles

Isaiah 41:1 *Keep silence before me, O islands; and let the people renew their strength: let them come near; then let them speak: let us come near together to judgment.*

CHAPTER 15

SPIRITUALITY

Spirituality is the commitment to religious values and sacred matters concerning the people who have been set apart for the services of God. In the New Testament a person is spiritual because of the indwelling presence and power of the Holy Spirit and the spiritual gifts which God imparts to the believer.

INTRODUCTION

Spirit is a word with three distinct meanings in the Bible:

1.   It is used as a general reference in the New Testament to give a description of the Spirit of human beings.

2.   Jesus made several specific references to His Spirit in a human sense.

3.   Paul sometimes referred to the spirit of those to whom he wrote.

1 Cor 15:44-46 *It is sown a natural body; it is raised a spiritual body. There is a natural body, and there is a spiritual body. [45] And so it is written, The first man Adam was made a living soul; the last Adam was made a quickening spirit. [46] Howbeit that was not first which is spiritual, but that which is natural; and afterward that which is spiritual.*

SPIRITUAL THINGS DISTINCT FROM EARTHLY GOODS

Romans 15:27 *It hath pleased them verily; and their debtors they are. For if the Gentiles have been made partakers of their spiritual things, their duty is also to minister unto them in carnal things.*

1 Cor 9:11 *If we have sown unto you spiritual things, is it a great thing if we shall reap your carnal things?*

1.   The Spirit gives the law.

Romans 7:14 *For we know that the law is spiritual: but I am carnal, sold under sin.*

2. The Spirit Supplied Israel with water and food.

1 Cor 10:3-4 *And did all eat the same spiritual meat; [4] And did all drink the same spiritual drink: for they drank of that spiritual Rock that followed them: and that Rock was Christ.*

3. We receive blessings from the Spirit

Eph 1:3 *Blessed be the God and Father of our Lord Jesus Christ, who hath blessed us with all spiritual blessings in heavenly places in Christ.*

4. The spirit helps us understand the truth.

1 Cor 2:13-15 *Which things also we speak, not in the words which man's wisdom teacheth, but which the Holy Ghost teacheth; comparing spiritual things with spiritual. [14] But the natural man receiveth not the things of the Spirit of God: for they are foolishness unto him: neither can he know them, because they are spiritually discerned. [15] But he that is spiritual judgeth all things, yet he himself is judged of no man.*

Col 1:9 *For this cause we also, since the day we heard it, do not cease to pray for you, and to desire that ye might be filled with the knowledge of his will in all wisdom and spiritual understanding.*

Rev 11:8 *And their dead bodies shall lie in the street of the great city, which spiritually is called Sodom and Egypt, where also our Lord was crucified.*

BE CONTROLLED BY THE SPIRIT

1 Cor 2:15 *But he that is spiritual judgeth all things, yet he himself is judged of no man.*

Gal 6:1 *Brethren, if a man be overtaken in a fault, ye which are spiritual, restore such an one in the spirit of meekness; considering thyself, lest thou also be tempted.*

Songs should be Sung in the Spirit

Eph 5:19 *Speaking to yourselves in psalms and hymns and spiritual songs, singing and making melody in your heart to the Lord.*

Col 3:16 *Let the word of Christ dwell in you richly in all wisdom; teaching and admonishing one another in psalms and hymns and spiritual songs, singing with grace in your hearts to the Lord.*

SPIRITUAL GIFTS

1 Cor 12:8-10 *For to one is given by the Spirit the word of wisdom: to another the word of knowledge by the same Spirit; [9] To another faith by the same Spirit; to another the gifts of healing by the same*

Spirit; [10] To another the working of miracles; to another prophecy; to another discerning of spirits: to another divers kinds of tongues; to another the interpretation of tongues.

1. Togues and Interpretation of Tongues are Similar

Eph 4:7-13 *But unto everyone of us is given grace according to the measure of the gift of Christ. [8] Wherefore he saith, When he ascended up on high, he led captivity captive, and gave gifts unto men. [9] (Now that he ascended, what is it but that he also descended first into the lower parts of the earth? [10] He that descended is the same also that ascended up far above all heavens, that he might fill all things.) [11] And he gave some, apostles; and some, prophets; and some, evangelists; and some, pastors and teachers; [12] For the perfecting of the saints, for the work of the ministry, for the edifying of the body of Christ. [13] Till we all come in the unity of the faith, and of the knowledge of the Son of God, unto a perfect man, unto the measure of the stature of the fullness of Christ.*

Romans 12:3-8 *For I say, through the grace given unto me, to every man that is among you, not to think of himself more highly than he ought to think; but to think soberly, according as God hath dealt to every man the measure of faith. [4] For as we have many members in one body, and all members have not the same office: [5] So we, being many, are one body in Christ, and every one members one of another. [6] Having then gifts differing according to the grace that is given to us, whether prophecy, let us prophesy according to the proportion of faith; [7] Or ministry, let us wait on our ministering: or he that teacheth, on teaching; [8] Or he that exhorteth, on exhortation: he that giveth, let him do it with simplicity; he that ruleth, with diligence; he that sheweth mercy, with cheerfulness.*

2. Gifts He Possesses

1 Cor 12:14 *For the body is not one member, but many.*

3. A Word of Comfort.

 Ephesiaps 6:10-11. A short prayer for strength. In praying any prayer, we must live according to the prayer we pray in order for it to work according to God's will. Jesus prayed that we all would be as one, even as He and the Father are one. He prayed that we would be kept from the evil of the world and for them that believe on Him through their own words. He even sanctified Himself that we would be sanctified (John 17:15,19-21). He prayed for them and not for the world (verse 9). *Finally my brethren, be strong in the Lord, and in the power of his might. Put on the whole armour of God, that you may be able to stand against the wiles of the devil (Ephesians 6:10-11).*

CHAPTER 16

THE REVELATION OF JESUS CHRIST

As John writes, he depicts worship in heaven and warfare on earth; and the Lord is the victor. No matter how dark the day or how strong the forces of evil, the Lamb of God wins the victory.

The key verse is 1:19. John was told to write the things which you have seen [Gospel of John, Chapter 1], and the things which are [Gospel of John, Chapters 2-3], and the things which will take place after this [Gospel of John, Chapter 4-22].

Revelation Chapters 6 through 19 parallel, which is saying to conform in direction with something else, which ,is found in Matthew 24 and Mark 13 in describing the day of the Lord or the Tribulation. The first part is described in Revelations Chapters 6 through 9; the middle in Chapters 10 through 14; and the last part (the great tribulation) in Chapters 15 through 19.

INTRODUCTION

The Revelation of Jesus Christ, which God gave unto him, to shew unto his servants things which must shortly come to pass; and he sent and signified it by his angel unto his servant John. (Revelation 1:1).

1.   Revelation is defined as to unveil or uncover. It implies the lifting up of a curtain so all can see alike what is uncovered. When applied to writing it means to reveal or make clear.

Eph 3:3 *IIow that by revelation he made known unto me the mystery; (as I wrote afore in few words.*

Gal 1:12 *For I neither received it of man, neither was I taught it, but by the revelation of Jesus Christ.*

2.   When revelation applied to a person, it denotes a visible presence.

Illustration: The question is who?

Rev 1:2 *Who bare record of the word of God, and of the testimony of Jesus Christ, and of all things that he saw.*

Rev 1:7 *Behold, he cometh with clouds; and every eye shall see him, and they also which pierced him: and all kindreds of the earth shall wail because of him. Even so, Amen.*

1 Pet 1: 7 *That the trial of your faith, being much more precious than of gold that perisheth, though it be tried with fire, might be found unto praise and honor and glory at the appearing of Jesus Christ.*

1 Pet 1:13 *Wherefore gird up the loins of your mind, be sober, and hope to the end for the grace that is to be brought unto you at the revelation of Jesus Christ.*

4.   Here it refers to both the book and the person of Christ. The illustration is found in 1 Corinthians 16:15. Here we understand that the chapter is talking about things concerning the house of Stephanas and other brethren. It is only being used as a illustration of a person.

5.   Reference to the person.

1 Cor 16:15-16 *I beseech you, brethren, (ye know the house of Stephanas, that it is the first fruits of Achaia, and that they have addicted themselves to the ministry of the saints), [16] That ye submit yourselves unto such, and to every one that helpeth with us and laboureth.*

6.   When we look at the word *revelation*, we really are talking about the word of God. This is what it was all about with John. He was talking about the word of God, and this is what was revealed unto him and he revealed it to us. Even now as we speak, I am giving to you the revelation of God, even though all I am just saying what he has here in the book.

Revelation Being Communicated

Gal 2:2 *And I went up by revelation, and communicated unto them that gospel which I preach among the Gentiles, but privately to them which were of reputation, lest by any means I should run, or had run, in vain.*

Paul compares this gospel of 14 years with that of other apostles and found that it was truth. We find this in the first verse. *Then fourteen years after I went up again to Jerusalem with Barnabas, and took Titus with me also* (Gal 2:1).

LIMITATION OF CHRIST'S POWER

A revelation altogether concerning Christ, but only one was from Him. Christ is not the main subject of the book. God gave it to Christ, emphasizing His limitation during His incarnation. To illustrate read Isaiah 50:4; Matthew 28:18; Mark 13:32; and Luke 1:40,52.

Isaiah 50:4 *The Lord GOD hath given me the tongue of the learned, that I should know how to speak a word in season to him that is weary: he wakeneth morning by morning, he wakeneth mine ear to hear as the learned.*

Matt 28:18 *And Jesus came and spake unto them, saying, All power is given unto me in heaven and in earth.*

Mark 13:32 *But of that day and that hour knoweth no man, no, not the angels which are in heaven, neither the Son, but the Father.*

Here is another illustration emphasizing God's power. This shows the power of God and helps us to understand what the Revelation of Him is all about. Look at this illustrated revelation in Luke 1:52.

Luke 1:52 *He hath put down the mighty from their seats, and exalted them of low degree.*

That Which Is In All Eternity

The purpose was to reveal, not to hide things from His servants, events from John's days into all eternity. Revelation 21:22, gives a very good illustration of all eternity.

Rev 21:22 *And I saw no temple therein: for the Lord God Almighty and the Lamb are the temple of it.*

NEW TESTAMENT REVELATIONS

1.   John's Commission to Write the Revelation

John tells what Christ looks like. *His head and his hairs were white like wool, as white as snow; and his eyes were as a flame of fire; [15] Christ's feet were like unto fine brass, as if they burned in a furnace; and His voice as the sound of many waters* (John 1:14-15).

The John emphasizes things or events: Events of the whole church age which is found in verses 1 through 3.

2.   The Whole Church

Rev 1:1-3 *The Revelation of Jesus Christ, which God gave unto him, to shew unto his servants things which must shortly come to pass; and he sent and signified it by his angel unto his servant John: [2] Who bare record of the word of God, and of the testimony of Jesus Christ, and of all things that he saw. [3] Blessed is he that readeth, and they that hear the words of this prophecy, and keep those things which are written therein: for the time is at hand.*

3.   Events in Heaven

Rev 1:4-5 *John to the seven churches which are in Asia: Grace be unto you, and peace, from him which is, and which was, and which is to come: and from the seven Spirits which are before his throne: [5]*

And from Jesus Christ, who is the faithful witness, and the first begotten of the dead, and the prince of the kings of the earth. Unto him that loved us, and washed us from our sins in his own blood.

TRIBULATION

Events of the future tribulation of Daniel's 70th week are found in Revelation 6 through 19. This brings us around to the 4th Events of the Millennium is in Revelation 20, which is the 5th event of the eternal new heavens and the new earth, which is in Revelation 21 through 22.

First we will study Revelations chapter 9 verses 1-3.

Rev 9:1 *And the fifth angel sounded, and I saw a star fall from heaven unto the earth: and to him was given the key of the bottomless pit. [2] And he opened the bottomless pit; and there arose a smoke out of the pit, as the smoke of a great furnace; and the sun and the air were darkened by reason of the smoke of the pit. [3] And there came out of the smoke locusts upon the earth: and unto them was given power, as the scorpions of the earth have power.*

1. The bottomless pit is the Abyss, the abode of evil spirits or demons.
2. The key represents authority.
3. Smoke from the pit indicates fires below.
4. Locust-like creatures come out of the smoke.

1. Fifth Trumpet Brings Torment to Unbelievers

Chapter 9 describes the first two woes coming after trumpets five and six. Keeping in mind that God is still in control of everything, the fifth trumpet brings a 5-month period of torment on the unbelievers of the earth.

Look at Rev 9:1. The fifth angel sounded and John saw a star fall from heaven unto the earth. This star could have been either an angel of God or Satan, the one who has authority over the pit. Please understand this. This is why we should be so careful in how we read this. Look at the word *{either}* . It could have been an angel or it could have been Satan.

2. The Mystery Star

Luke 10:18 says, *And he said unto them, I beheld Satan as lightning fall from heaven.*

A further reference to the mystery star is given in Rev 1:20. *The mystery of the seven stars which thou sawest in my right hand, and the seven golden candlesticks. The seven stars are the angels of the seven churches: and the seven candlesticks which thou sawest are the seven churches.*

Rev 20:1 *And I saw an angel come down from heaven, having the key of the bottomless pit and a great chain in his hand.*

In verse 1, the key was given to the bottomless pit, even though he who it was given, God still had the control.

3.   Author of Power

Luke 8:31 *And they besought him that he would not command them to go out into the deep.*

4.   The Key to the Bottomless Pit

Rev 9:11 *And they had a king over them, which is the angel of the bottomless pit, whose name in the Hebrew tongue is Abaddon, but in the Greek tongue hath his name Apollyon.*

5.   Lucifer, the Son of Morning

Isaiah 14:12 questions Lucifer, *How art thou fallen from heaven, O Lucifer, son of the morning! How art thou cut down to the ground, which didst weaken the nations!*

Reasons are given in the next two verses. Isaiah 14:13-14 *For thou hast said in thine heart, I will ascend into heaven, I will exalt my throne above the stars of God: I will sit also upon the mount of the congregation, in the sides of the north: [14]Yet thou shalt be brought down to hell, to the sides of the pit.*

He opened the bottomless pit. Rev 9:2 *And he opened the bottomless pit; and there arose a smoke out of the pit, as the smoke of a great furnace; and the sun and the air were darkened by reason of the smoke of the pit.* The bottomless pit is the Abyss, the abode of evil spirits or demons.

EVIL SPIRITS AND DEMONS

Luke 8:30-31 And Jesus asked him, saying, What is thy name? And he said, Legion: because many devils were entered into him. [31] And they besought him that he would not command them to go out into the deep.

When the bottomless pit was opened Locust-like creatures came out of the smoke.

- The bottomless pit is the Abyss, the abode of evil spirits or demons.
- The key represents authority.
- Smoke from the pit indicates fires below.
- Locust-like creatures came out of the smoke.

1. Rev. 9:2 describes locust like creatures coming out of the smoke. They are not literal locusts but symbols of destruction. In the Old Testament, locusts are symbols of destruction because they just eat up and do away with everything. It makes it easy for people to understand, for they know what the locusts can do.

2. God also used locusts to show His power and control over Pharaoh.

Deut 28:42 *All thy trees and fruit of thy land shall the locust consume.*

3. These are the things that are going to take place during the Tribulation times. There are many other illustrations that will help to understand.

1 Kings 8:37 *If there be in the land famine, if there be pestilence, blasting, mildew, locust, or if there be caterpillar; if their enemy besiege them in the land of their cities; whatsoever plague, whatsoever sickness there be.*

Ps 78:46 *He gave also their increase unto the caterpillar, and their labour unto the locust.*

Joel 2:11 *And the LORD shall utter his voice before his army: for his camp is very great: for he is strong that executeth his word: for the day of the LORD is great and very terrible; and who can abide it?* (KJV)

4. Considering the identity of their king and the Abyss from which they come, these locusts probably represent demons and, like scorpions, they can hurt people. They are to not harm the vegetation, as the locusts would, but only the men who do not belong to God. Rev 9:4-6 commanded that they are not to hurt the grass, any green things, not even a tree, only people who don't have the seal of God on their forehead. They are not allowed to kill any thing at this point. They are only to torment unbelievers for five months. The pain will be like that of a scorpion and the torment will be so great that they will desire to die. But part of the judgment will be that men cannot die to escape it.

Rev 9:4-6 *And it was commanded them that they should not hurt the grass of the earth, neither any green thing, neither any tree; but only those men which have not the seal of God in their foreheads. [5] And to them it was given that they should not kill them, but that they should be tormented five months: and their torment was as the torment of a scorpion, when he striketh a man. [6] And in those days shall men seek death, and shall not find it; and shall desire to die, and death shall flee from them.*

5. The description of the locusts indicates that they are demons that are given physical form in order to manifest their destruction and torment.

Rev 9:7 *And the shapes of the locusts were like unto horses prepared unto battle; and on their heads were as it were crowns like gold, and their faces were as the faces of men.*

6. The description includes feminine hair perhaps make them seductive and attractive. Here again we have a word that will go either way or any way, the bottom of it all, we don't really know.

Rev 9:8 *And they had hair as the hair of women, and their teeth were as the teeth of lions.*

7.   However they will have teeth like lions. Another scripture with similar phrasing is Joel 1:6. The teeth of lions shows them to be destructive and hurtful.

Joel 1:6 *For a nation is come up upon my land, strong, and without number, whose teeth are the teeth of a lion, and he hath the cheek teeth of a great lion.*

8.   The breastplates of iron will make them indestructible. Their wings symbolize swiftness.

Rev 9:9 *And they had breastplates, as it were breastplates of iron; and the sound of their wings was as the sound of chariots of many horses running to battle.*

9.   The venom from their stings give them the power to hurt. Fortunately for mankind, their period of torment is limited to five months. But the next judgment is even worse.

Rev 9:10 *And they had tails like unto scorpions, and there were stings in their tails: and their power was to hurt men five months.*

KING OVER THE DEMONS

The king over these demons is apparently Satan, who is given temporary authority over the Abyss. The name Abaddon is Hebrew for Destruction

Rev 9:11 *And they had a king over them, which is the angel of the bottomless pit, whose name in the Hebrew tongue is Abaddon, but in the Greek tongue hath his name Apollyon.*

Job 28:22 *Destruction and death say, We have heard the fame thereof with our ears.*

Prov 15:11 *Hell and destruction are before the LORD: how much more then the hearts of the children of men?*

Prov 27:20 *Hell and destruction are never full; so the eyes of man are never satisfied.*

SIXTH TRUMPET: DEATH TO A THIRD OF NONBELIEVERS

1.   Two more woes are to follow. As the end approaches, the intensity and severity of the trumpet judgment increases.

Rev 9:12 *One woe is past; and, behold, there come two woes more hereafter.*

2.   The sixth trumpet results in the death of the third surviving unbelievers on the earth.

Rev 9:13 *And the sixth angel sounded, and I heard a voice from the four horns of the golden altar which is before God.*

3.   The four horns of the golden altar which is before God are the angel with the prayers of the saints.

Rev 8:3 And another angel came and stood at the altar, having a golden censer; and there was given unto him much incense, that he should offer it with the prayers of all saints upon the golden altar which was before the throne.

4.   The four bound angels are fallen angels or demons who had been temporarily bound by God.

Rev 9:14 Saying to the sixth angel which had the trumpet, Loose the four angels which are bound in the great river Euphrates.

5.   Scripture also refers to the great river Euphrates in Genesis 15:18.

Gen 15:18 In the same day the LORD made a covenant with Abram, saying, Unto thy seed have I given this land, from the river of Egypt unto the great river, the river Euphrates.

6.   The four bound angels will be loosed for the purpose of killing a third of the population of the world. They appear to be in charge of the horde of demonic horsemen who will actually accomplish the massacre.

Rev 9:15 And the four angels were loosed, which were prepared for an hour, and a day, and a month, and a year, for to slay the third part of men.

7.   In Revelation 9:16-19, John talks about hearing the number of the horsemen: which was 200,000,000 literally, *two myriads of myriads* although the majority of manuscripts reads *a myriad of myriads*, or 100,000,000. There is other scriptural reference to these numbers.

Rev 5:11 And I beheld, and I heard the voice of many angels round about the throne and the beasts and the elders: and the number of them was ten thousand times ten thousand, and thousands of thousands.

Ps 68:17 The chariots of God are twenty thousand, even thousands of angels: the Lord is among them, as in Sinai, in the holy place.

Dan 7:10 A fiery stream issued and came forth from before him: thousand thousands ministered unto him, and ten thousand times ten thousand stood before him: the judgment was set, and the books were opened.

8.   John had no time to count such a large army. The riders (and perhaps the horses) wore breastplates. An armored cavalry was always a most formidable opponent.

Rev 9:16 And the number of the army of the horsemen were two hundred thousand thousand: and I heard the number of them.

FIRE, SMOKE, AND BRIMSTONE

1.   The fire, smoke, and brimstone are three separate plagues, which together will kill a third of mankind. In light of their description, and the fact that they are ruled by four fallen angels, these horses and riders are probably demons as well. The demons of the fifth trumpet do not kill (Rev 9:1-6), but these demons riders do kill. The power to kill is in their mouth, from which come the fire, smoke, and brimstone. Their tails have heads like serpents, with the power to hurt people. This sixth trumpet (Rev 9:18) combined with the trumpet of the fourth seal (Rev 6:8) reduces the population of the earth to one-half of its pre-Tribulation level.

Rev 9:17 *And thus I saw the horses in the vision, and them that sat on them, having breastplates of fire, and of jacinth, and brimstone: and the heads of the horses were as the heads of lions and out of their mouths issued fire and smoke and brimstone.*

2.   The trumpet of the fourth seal (Rev 6:8) and sixth trumpet bring death to nonbelievers.

Rev 6:8 *And I looked, and behold a pale horse: and his name that sat on him was Death, and Hell followed with him. And power was given unto them over the fourth part of the earth, to kill with sword, and with hunger, and with death, and with the beasts of the earth.*

Rev 9:18 *By these three was the third part of men killed, by the fire, and by the smoke, and by the brimstone, which issued out of their mouths.*

THE UNREPENTANT WORSHIP IDOLS

1.   By this point in the Tribulation period, most surviving unbelievers will have permanently made up their minds concerning Christ. They will refuse to repent, even under this terrible judgment.

Rev 9:20-21 *And the rest of the men which were not killed by these plagues yet repented not of the works of their hands, that they should not worship devils, and idols of gold, and silver, and brass, and stone, and of wood: which neither can see, nor hear, nor walk. [21] Neither repented they of their murders, nor of their sorceries, nor of their fornication, nor of their thefts.*

2.   Their religious activities will involve worship of idols and demons (devils), and sorceries or witchcraft, with the use of magic potions. Idolatry is in fact the worship of demons. Of grave concern to the apostle is that behind the idols are fallen angels, evil spirits.

1 Cor 10:20 *But I say, that the things which the Gentiles sacrifice, they sacrifice to devils, and not to God: and I would not that ye should have fellowship with devils.*

3.   This is in keeping with Deuteronomy 32:17 and Psalm 96:5.

Deut 32:17 *They sacrificed unto devils, not to God; to gods whom they knew not, to new gods that came newly up, whom your fathers feared not.*

Psa 96:5 *For all the gods of the nations are idols: but the LORD made the heavens.*

4. Since Paul has already established that these religious feasts involved fellowship with the altar, if the Corinthians attend a heathen feast, they will be having fellowship with devils. This is reference to 1 Cor 10:20.

5. Three of the four sins listed in 1 Cor 10:21 are specifically prohibited by the Ten Commandments (Exodus 20:3-17). For sorceries, compare them with also Exodus 18:23, 21:8, 22:15 and Galatians 5:20. Here is just one reference.

Gal 5:20 Idolatry, witchcraft, hatred, variance, emulations, wrath, strife, seditions, heresies.

THE BOTTOMLESS PIT

1. John employs the image of a pit seven times in Revelation to describe hell (verses 2 and 11; 11:7; 17:8; 20:1 and 3). Each time, the pit is closely associated with demons; it is also associated with the unsaved (Romans 10:7). This image of hell may also imply darkness and imprisonment since pits were often used as prisons in ancient cultures.

2. The word obviously which is easily discovered, seen or understood. The pit appears as a place of suffering. If you have trouble believing God could ever make a hell, remember it was prepared for the Devil and his angels, and we find reference to it in Matthew 25:41.

3. Those who go to hell are in essence choosing to spend eternity with Satan rather than with Christ. See Revelation 9:1-12; Genesis 2:17; and Luke 16:23-25.

Rev. 3:11 *Hold fast to what you have, that no man take your crown.*

Rev. 3:16 *Because you are neither cold nor hot, I will spew you out of my mouth.*

Rev. 16:15 *Blessed are they that watch and keep their garment, lest they walk naked and shame.*

Rev. 21:8 *All who sin will have their part in the lake of fire.*

Rev. 22:19 *If any man take away from the words of this book, God shall take away his part out of the book of life.*

CHAPTER 17

COMMITMENT TO RELIGIOUS VALUES

Spiritual things are distinct from earthly goods and include a sensitivity or commitment to religious values and matters.

THE HOLY SPIRIT DWELLS WITHIN

1. In the New Testament a person is spiritual because of the indwelling presence and power of the Holy Spirit and the spiritual gifts which God has imparted to the believer as in 1 Cor 12:1 and Col 1:9.

John 14:17 *Even the Spirit of truth; whom the world cannot receive, because it seeth him not, neither knoweth him: but ye know him; for he dwelleth with you, and shall be in you.*

2. But the most important use of the word is in reference to the Holy Spirit. The spirit gave the law according to the Bible and it supplied Israel with water and food.

3. The Christian's every blessing is from the spirit as is his understanding of the truth and the ability to understand the Scripture (1 Cor 2:13-15; Col 1:9).

4. Christian's songs should be sung in the spirit (Eph 5:19; Col 3:16).

5. The Christian should be so controlled by the Spirit that he can be called spiritual (1 Cor 2:25 and Gal 6:1). This is what being spiritual is all about--being controlled by the Holy Spirit in a way you can become spiritual according to the word of God.

SPIRITUAL GIFTS OF INDIVIDUALS

1. In the New Testament a person is spiritual because of the indwelling presence and power of the Holy Spirit and the Spiritual gifts which God imparts to the believer (1 Cor 12:1; Col 1:9).

2. According to the Bible, Spiritual gifts are bestowed upon a Christian by the Holy Spirit for the purpose of building up the church. The list of Spiritual gifts is found in 1 Cor 12:8-10.

SPIRITUAL GIFTS OF THE CHURCH

1. Special gifts are bestowed upon Christians by the Holy Spirit for the purpose of building up the church. Again we find them in 1 Corinthians 12:8-10: wisdom, knowledge, faith, healing, miracles, prophecy, discerning of spirits, speaking in tongues, and interpretation of tongues. There are similar lists appearing in Ephesians and Romans. These gifts are equally valid but not equally valuable. Their value is determined by their work to the church. In dealing with this matter, he used the human body. All members of the body have functions but some are more important than others.

2. The service of each Christian should be in proportion to the gifts which he possesses. Since these gifts are gifts of grace, according to the Bible their use must be controlled by the principle of love of the spirit

The Holy Spirit Inspired the Prophets

Acts 2:17-21 *And it shall come to pass in the last days, saith God, I will pour out of my spirit upon all flesh: and your sons and your daughters shall prophesy, and your young men shall see visions, and your old men shall dream dreams: [18] And on my servants and on my handmaidens I will pour out in those days of my Spirit; and they shall prophesy: [19] And I will shew wonders in heaven above, and signs in the earth beneath; blood, and fire, and vapour of smoke: [20] The sun shall be turned into darkness, and the moon into blood, before that great and notable day of the Lord come: [21] And it shall come to pass, that whosoever shall call on the name of the Lord shall be saved.*

Acts 2:4 *And they were all filled with the Holy Ghost, and began to speak with other tongues, as the spirit gave them utterance.*

Acts 19:6 *And when Paul had laid his hands upon them, the Holy Ghost came on them; and they spake with tongues, and prophesied.*

The Holy Spirit Given to New Christians

Acts 10:44-48 *While Peter yet spake these words, the Holy Ghost fell on all them which heard the word. [45] And they of the circumcision which believed were astonished, as many as came with Peter, because that on the Gentiles also was poured out the gift of the Holy Ghost. [46] For they heard them speak with tongues, and magnify God. Then answered Peter, [47] Can any man forbid water, that these should not be baptized, which have received the Holy Ghost as well as we? [48] And he commanded them to be baptized in the name of the Lord.*

Fulfilled and Sanctified

2 Cor 3:18 *But we all, with open face beholding as in a glass the glory of the Lord, are changed into the same image from glory to glory, even as by the Spirit of the Lord.*

2 Thes 2:13 *But we are bound to give thanks always to God for you, brethren beloved of the Lord, because God hath from the beginning chosen you to salvation through sanctification of the Spirit and belief of the truth.*

Direction of Christian Missionary

Acts 10:19-20 *While Peter thought on the vision, the Spirit said unto him, Behold, three men seek thee. [20] Arise therefore, and get thee down, and go with them, doubting nothing: for I have sent them.*

Acts 16:6-7 *Now when they had gone throughout Phrygia and the region of Galatia, and were forbidden of the Holy Ghost to preach the word in Asia, [7] After they were come to Mysia, they assayed to go into Bithynia: but the Spirit suffered them not.*

Through the Spirit we belong to Jesus Christ

The Holy Spirit is the Spirit of Jesus Christ. A person can relate to Him only by means of the Holy Spirit. In the Gospel of John, He is called the Helper.

2 Cor 3:17 *Now the Lord is that Spirit: and where the spirit of the Lord is, there is liberty.*

Romans 8:9 *But ye are not in the flesh, but in the Spirit, if so be that the Spirit of God dwell in you. Now if any man have not the Spirit of Christ, he is none of his.*

Gal 4:6 *And because ye are sons, God hath sent forth the Spirit of his Son into your hearts, crying, Abba, Father.*

The Holy Spirit is the Helper

John 14:16 *And I will pray the Father, and he shall give you another Comforter, that he may abide with you for ever.*

THE HOLY SPIRIT IS ACTIVE AMONG GOD'S PEOPLE

In the New Testament, the Holy Spirit was more active in the presence of God's people. The Holy Spirit was the agent of fulfillment of the Old Testament prophecies, and continued to inspire Christian prophets and works in order to work His will on earth. The Holy Spirit came upon new Christians in a way that purified and sanctified them and guided the direction of the early Christians missionary work.

The Holy Spirit Enables Man

The Spirit also refers to the Spirit of God, the Holy spirit in the Old Testament. The Spirit comes upon people to give them power to do God's will or to enable them to serve God in a special way.

1. Spirit of the Lord enabled Samson to kill a young lion with his bare hands.

Judges 14:5-6 *Then went Samson down, and his father and his mother, to Timnath, and came to the vineyards of Timnath: and, behold, a young lion roared against him. [6] And the Spirit of the LORD came mightily upon him, and he rent him as he would have rent a kid, and he had nothing in his hand: but he told not his father or his mother what he had done.*

2. Spirit of God gave Bezaleel the wisdom and skill to build the tabernacle.

Exodus 31:3 *And I have filled him with the spirit of God, in wisdom, and in understanding, and in knowledge, and in all manner of workmanship.*

3. Spirit of the Lord also enabled judges to lead Israel to military victory and the prophets to prophesy.

Judges 3:10 *And the spirit of the LORD came upon him, and he judged Israel, and went out to war: and the LORD delivered Chushan-rishatha'im king of Mesopotamia into his hand; and his hand prevailed against Chushan-rishatha'im.*

4. The spirit enabled the prophets to prophesy

Ezek 11:5 *And the Spirit of the LORD fell upon me, and said unto me, Speak; Thus saith the LORD; Thus have ye said, O house of Israel: for I know the things that come into your mind, everyone of them.*

5. The spirit served as God's agent to fulfill Old Testament prophesy.

Acts 1:16 *Men and brethren, this scripture must needs have been fulfilled, which the Holy Ghost by the mouth of David spake before concerning Judas, which was guide to them that took Jesus.*

Acts 2:16 *But this is that which was spoken by the prophet Joel.*

The Human Spirit

Scripture makes specific references to the spirit of man.

Matt 5:3 *Blessed are the poor in spirit: for theirs is the kingdom of heaven.*

Romans 8:16 *The Spirit itself beareth witness with our spirit, that we are the children of God.*

4:12 *For the word of God is quick, and powerful, and sharper than any two edged sword, piercing even to the dividing asunder of soul and spirit, and of the joints and marrow, and is a discerner of the thoughts and intents of the heart.*

Jesus Acknowledged His Human Spirit

Mark 2:8 *And immediately when Jesus perceived in his spirit that they so reasoned within themselves, he said unto them, Why reason ye these things in your hearts?*

John 11:33 *When Jesus therefore saw her weeping, and the Jews also weeping which came with her, he groaned in the spirit, and was troubled.*

Paul Referred to the Spirit in His Letter

Acts 17:16 *Now while Paul waited for them at Athens, his spirit was stirred in him, when he saw the city wholly given to idolatry.*

2 Cor 2:13 *I had no rest in my spirit, because I found not Titus my brother: but taking my leave of them, I went from thence into Macedonia.*

Gal 6:18 *Brethren, the grace of our Lord Jesus Christ be with your spirit. Amen.*

2 Tim 4:22 *The Lord Jesus Christ be with thy spirit. Grace be with you. Amen.*

GOOD AND EVIL SPIRITS

1. According to the Bible, the second common usage of the word spirit is in reference to good and evil, meaning human beings other than God's Spirit. The Bible also contains many references to evil spirit.

Psalms 104:4 *Who maketh his angels spirits; his ministers a flaming fire.*

2. The Bible also contains many references to evil spirits.

Mark 9:25 *When Jesus saw that the people came running together, he rebuked the foul spirit, saying unto him, Thou dumb and deaf spirit, I charge thee, come out of him, and enter no more into him.*

Acts 19:13-17 *Then certain of the vagabond Jews, exorcists, took upon them to call over them which had evil spirits the name of the Lord Jesus, saying, We adjure you by Jesus whom Paul preacheth. [14] And there were seven sons of one Sceva, a Jew, and chief of the priests, which did so. [15] And the evil spirit answered and said, Jesus I know, and Paul I know; but who are ye? [16] And the man in whom the evil spirit was leaped on them, and overcame them, and prevailed against them, so that they fled out of that house naked and wounded. [17] And this was known to all the Jews and Greeks also dwelling at Ephesus; and fear fell on them all, and the name of the Lord Jesus was magnified.*

Rev 18:2 *And he cried mightily with a strong voice, saying, Babylon the great is fallen, and is become the habitation of devils, and the hold of every foul spirit, and cage of every unclean and hateful bird.*

SUFFERING AND RENEWING

1 Peter 3:19-20 *By which also he went and preached unto the spirit in person. Which were sometimes disobedient, when the longsuffering of God waited in the days of Noah, while the ark was a preparing, wherein few, that is eight souls were saved by water.*

CHAPTER 18

SATAN'S REBELLION AGAINST GOD

Scriptural Teaching of Evil Spirits and Demons

The New Testament accepts the Old Testament teaching about demons and advances the doctrine significantly. Demons are designated in a number of different ways in the New Testament.

1.   Because the Jews believed God's power was unlimited, the Old Testament contains little information about demons. However, there is sufficient description of Satan's rebellion against God and the consequences for mankind.

Rev 12:9 *And the great dragon was cast out, that old serpent, called the Devil, and Satan, which deceiveth the whole world: he was cast out into the earth, and his angels were cast out with him.*

2.   Satan and his followers contaminated the human race with wickedness. The group that participated in the fall followed one of their own—Satan. The fall occurred before God's creation of the world, leaving Satan and his angels free to contaminate the human race with wickedness.

Gen 3:1 *Now the serpent was more subtle than any beast of the field which the LORD God had made. And he said unto the woman, Yea, hath God said, Ye shall not eat of every tree of the garden?*

Gen 6:4-5 *There were giants in the earth in those days; and also after that, when the sons of God came in unto the daughters of men, and they bare children to them, the same became mighty men which were of old, men of renown. [5] And GOD saw that the wickedness of man was great in the earth, and that every imagination of the thoughts of his heart was only evil continually.*

3.   God punished wickedness and evil. According to scripture, Matthew is saying to them that sat on the left hand, *Depart from me, you cursed into everlasting fire.* Only part of the fallen angels took part in the wickedness at the time of the flood.

Judges 6:1 *And the children of Israel did evil in the sight of the LORD: and the LORD delivered them into the hand of Midian seven years.*

1 Peter 3:19-20 *By which also he went and preached unto the spirit in person. [20] Which were sometimes disobedient, when the longsuffering of God waited in the days of Noah, while the ark was a preparing, wherein few, that is eight souls were saved by water.*

2 Pet 2: 4 *For if God spared not the angels that sinned, but cast them down to hell, and delivered them into chains of darkness, to be reserved unto judgment.*

A Symbolic View of the Fall

1. A symbolic view of the beginning of the fall appears in Revelation where the dragon (a symbol for Satan) *drew a third of the stars of heaven* (a symbol for angels) and *threw them to the earth.*

Rev 12:3-4 *And there appeared another wonder in heaven; and behold a great red dragon having seven heads and ten horns, and seven crowns upon his heads. [4] And his tail drew the third part of the stars of heaven, and did cast them to the earth: and the dragon stood before the woman which was ready to be delivered, for to devour her child as soon as it was born.*

2. Satan has his own following of angels; presumably these are demons according to Matthew's saying, *Depart from me, you cursed, into everlasting fire prepared for the devil and his angels.*

Rev 12:9 *And the great dragon was cast out, that old serpent, called the Devil, and Satan, which deceiveth the whole world: he was cast out into the earth, and his angels were cast out with him.*

An Evil Spirit Tormented Saul

1. The primitive status of the understanding of demons during this time is reflected in the way the Old Testament relates to the fallen angels of God. It was a *distressing or an evil spirit from God.*

2. Samuel talked about the time when an evil spirit would come from God that would bring great distress to Saul the king. It was a lying spirit from the Lord about whom Micah, the prophet of the Lord, also spoke.

1 Sam 16:15-16 *And Saul's servants said unto him, Behold now, an evil spirit from God troubleth thee. [16] Let our lord now command thy servants, which are before thee, to seek out a man, who is a cunning player on an harp: and it shall come to pass, when the evil spirit from God is upon thee, that he shall play [music] with his hand, and thou shalt be well.*

1 Sam 16:23 *And it came to pass, when the evil spirit from God was upon Saul, that David took a harp, and played with his hand: so Saul was refreshed, and was well, and the evil spirit departed from him.*

Pagan Worship

Pagan is a word you seldom find in the New Testament, because pagan worship is also related to demon activity in the Old Testament. Demons delight in making heathen idols which are the focus of their activities. In the New Testament it is the same. The difference is the changing of their names; their activities are still the same.

Lev 17:7 *And they shall no more, offer their sacrifices unto devils, after whom they have gone a whoring. This shall be a statute forever unto them throughout their generations.*

Psalms 106:37 *Yea, they sacrificed their sons and their daughters unto devils.*

1 Tim 4:1 *Now the Spirit speaketh expressly, that in the latter times some shall depart from the faith, giving heed to seducing spirits, and doctrines of devils.*

THE EARTHLY MINISTRY OF JESUS

1. A primary purpose of Jesus' earthly ministry was to overcome the power of Satan. According to the Bible, this included His conquest of the demonic realm. This explains the conflict between Jesus and these evil spirits while He was on the earth.

Matt 12:25-29 *And Jesus knew their thoughts and said unto them, Every kingdom divided against itself is brought to desolation; and every city or house divided against itself shall not stand: [26] And if Satan cast out Satan, he is divided against himself; how shall then his kingdom stand? [27] And if I by Beelzubub cast out devils, by whom do your children cast them out? therefore they shall be your judges. [28] But if I cast out devihs by the spirit of God, then the kingdom of God is come unto you. [29] Or else how can one enter into a strong man's house, and spoil his goods, except he first bind the strongman? and then he will spoil his house.*

John 12:31-33 *Now is the judgment of this world: now shall the prince of this world be cast out. [32] And I, if I be lifted up from the earth, will draw all men unto me. [33] This he said, signifying what death he should die.*

John 3:8 *The wind bloweth where it listeneth, and thou hearest the sound thereof, but canst not tell whence it cometh, and whither it goeth: so is everyone that is born of the Spirit.*

Jesus Accused by Enemies

2. Yet Jesus' enemies accused Him of being in alliance with Satan's kingdom, including his demons. This same accusation was made against His forerunner, John the Baptist. But Jesus' works of goodness and righteousness showed that these claims were not true.

Mark 3:22 *And the scribes which came down from Jerusalem said: He hath Beelzebub, and by the prince of the devils casteth he out devils.*

John 8:48 *Then answered the Jews, and said unto him, Say we not well that thou art a Samaritan, and hast a devil?*

John the Baptist Accused by Enemies

3.   This same accusation was made against His forerunner, John the Baptist. But Jesus' works of goodness and righteousness showed that these claims were not true.

Matt 11:18 *For John came neither eating nor drinking, and they say, He hath a devil.*

Luke 7:33 *For John the Baptist came neither eating bread nor drinking wine; and ye say, He hath a devil.*

New Testament Reference to Evil Spirit

3.   Quite frequently in the New Testament, they are called unclean spirits. Another descriptive phrase for them is wicked or evil spirit. In some of Paul's writings, he calls them deceiving spirit. John refers to them the spirit of error and spirits of demons. In 1-John and Revelation, Luke describes one demon as a spirit of divination. We can see how the word demon has advanced. No matter how advanced the word is, the activities are the same as evil spirit, or spirit of error.

Matt 10:1 *And when he had called unto him his twelve disciples, he gave them power against unclean spirits, to cast them out, and to heal all manner of sickness and all manner of disease.*

Mark 6:7 *And he called unto him the twelve, and began to send, them forth by two and two; and gave them power over unclean spirits.*

Luke 7:21 *And in that same hour he cured many of their infirmities and plagues, and of evil spirits; and unto many that were blind he gave sight.*

Acts 19:12-13 *So that from his body were brought unto the sick handkerchiefs or aprons, and the diseases departed from them, and the evil spirits went out of them. [13] Then certain of the vagabond Jews, exorcists, took upon them to call over them which had evil spirits the name of the Lord Jesus, saying, We adjure you by Jesus whom Paul preacheth.*

1 Tim 4:1 *Now the Spirit speaketh expressly, that in the latter times some shall depart from the faith, giving heed to seducing spirits, and doctrines of devils.*

1 John 4:6 We are of God: he that knoweth God heareth us; he that is not of God heareth not us. Hereby know we the spirit of truth, and the spirit of error.

Demonic Activities after the Resurrection of Jesus

4.   Following the resurrection of Jesus Christ and His return to heaven, demonic principalities and powers have continued their warfare against those who are Jesus followers.

Romans 8:38-39 *For I am persuaded, that neither death, nor life, nor angels, nor principalities, nor powers, nor things present, nor things to come; [39] Nor height, nor depth, nor any other creature, shall be able to separate us from the love of God, which is in Christ Jesus our Lord.*

Eph 11:12 *For we wrestle not against flesh and blood, but against principalities, against powers, against the rulers of, the darkness of this world, against spiritual wickedness in high places.*

1 Tim 4:1 *Now the Spirit speaketh expressly, that in the latter times some shall depart from the faith, giving heed to seducing spirits, and doctrines of devils.*

Acts 16:16 *And it came to pass, as we went to prayer, a certain damsel possessed with a spirit of divination met us, which brought her masters much gain by soothsaying.*

Rev 16:14 *For they are the spirits of devils, working miracles, which go forth unto the kings of the earth and of the whole world, to gather them to the battle of that great day of God Almighty.*

SATAN, KING OF THE BOTTOMLESS PIT

1.   The only individual demon name in the New Testament, Satan himself never is referred to as a demon. New Testament Revelation, calls him Abaddon which is in Hebrew, but in the Greek tongue he has the name Apollyon. There is strong evidence he has kingly authority of Legion, a collective name for a group of demons rather the name of a single demon.

Rev 9:11 *And they had a king over them, which is the angel of the bottomless pit, whose name in the Hebrew tongue is Abaddon, but in the Greek tongue hath his name Apollyon.*

Matt 8:29 *And, behold, they cried out, saying, What have we to do with thee, Jesus, thou Son of God? art thou come hither to torment us before the time?*

Mark 5: 9 *And he asked him, What is thy name? And he answered, saying, My name is Legion: for we are many.*

Luke 8:30 *And Jesus asked him, saying, What is thy name? And he said, Legion: because many devils were entered into him.*

Satan Overthrown

2.   Yet Satan and his allies will finally be overthrown by God. After Christ returns, the devil and his angels will be defeated/and thrown into the lake of fire and brimstone. This is a doom

with which demons are quite familiar. God will achieve the ultimate victory in this conflict which has been going on since the beginning of time.

Matt 25:41 *Then shall he say also unto them on the left hand, Depart from me, ye cursed, into everlasting fire, prepared for the devil and his angels.*

Matt 8:29 *And, behold, they cried out, saying, What have we to do with thee, Jesus, thou Son of God? art thou come hither to torment us before the time?*

GOD WILL ACHIEVE THE ULTIMATE VICTORY IN THIS CONFLICT WHICH HAS BEEN GOING ON SINCE THE BEGINNING OF TIME.

That they all may be one; as you, Father, art in me, and I in you, that they also may be one in us: that the world may believe that you hast sent me (John 17:21).

UNIT IV:
THE
CRUCIFIXION
OF
JESUS CHRIST

Crucifixion was used by many nations of the ancient world, including Assyria, Media, and Persia. Alexander the Great of Greece crucified 2,000 inhabitants of Tyre when he captured the city. The Romans later adopted this form of execution and used it often throughout their empire. Crucifixion was the Romans' most severe form of execution so it was reserved only for slaves and criminals. No Roman citizen could be crucified.

To the Jewish people, crucifixion represented the most disgusting form of death, yet the Jewish Sanhedrin sought and obtained Roman authorization to have Jesus crucified. The crucifixion of Jesus Christ was torture and execution used by the Romans to put Christ to death. However, out of the ugliness and agony of crucifixion God accomplished the greatest good of all the redemption of sinners.

CHAPTER 19

CRUCIFIXION

Crucifixion was used by many nations of the ancient world, including Assyria, Media, and Persia. Alexander the Great of Greece crucified 2,000 inhabitants of Tyre when he captured the city. The Romans later adopted this form of execution and used it often throughout their empire. Crucifixion was the Romans' most severe form of execution so it was reserved only for slaves and criminals. No Roman citizen could be crucified.

1. It was common in biblical times for the bodies of the executed to be publicly displayed by hanging them from the stake of the stockade wall. This was done to discourage civil disobedience and to mock defeated military foes. This practice may explain how the stake came to be used as an instrument of civil and military punishment.

Gen 40:19 *Yet within three days shall Pharaoh lift up thy head from off thee, and shall hang thee on a tree; and the birds shall eat thy flesh from off thee.*

2. Later such stakes came to be used with crossbeams as instruments of humiliation, torture, and execution for those who were convicted as enemies of the state, foreign soldiers, rebels and spies, and civil criminals such as thieves. It was followed by the further degrading practice most often used throughout the ancient world to then allow the victim to rot in public.

1 Sam 31:8 *And it came to pass on the morrow, when the Philistines came to strip the slain, that they found Saul and his three sons fallen in Mount Gilboa.*

1 Sam 31:9 *And they cut off his head, and stripped off his armor, and sent into the land of the Philistines round about, to publish it in the house of their idols, and among the people.*

1 Sam 31:10 *And they put his armor in the house of Ashtaroth: and they fastened his body to the wall of Bethshan.*

1 Sam 31:11 *And when the inhabitants of Jabesh-gilead heard of that which the Philistines had done to Saul;*

1 Sam 31:12 *All the valiant men arose, and went all night, and took the body of Saul and the bodies of his sons from the wall of Bethshan, and came to Jabesh, and burnt them there.*

1 Sam 31:13 *And they took their bones, and buried them under a tree at Jabesh, and fasted seven days.*

COMMON STYLES OF CROSSES

Ancient writers do not tell us much about how execution on a stake or cross was carried out. The scholars are not certain when a crossbeam was added to the simple stake. However, Jeremiah's mention of princes being "hung up by their hands" by the Babylonians may refer to the use of a crossbeam. Over time the simple pointed stake first used for execution was modified. Four styles of crosses were adopted.

1. The Latin cross shaped like a lower case "t" on which it is likely that Jesus died because they hung the sign "King of the Jews" above his head.

2. The St. Anthony's cross has the cross beam at the top shaped like a capital "T."

3. The St. Andrew's cross which is shaped like a capital "X."

4. The so-called Greek cross which has the crossbeam in the center shaped like a plus "+" sign.

JEWISH LAW DIRECTED DEATH BY STONING

1. In the ancient world during the Old Testament time, there is no evidence that the Jews fastened people to a stake or a cross as a means of execution. The law directed death by stoning.

Lev 20:2 *Again, thou shalt say to the children of Israel, Whosoever he be of the children of Israel, or of the strangers that sojourn in Israel, that giveth any of his seed unto Molech; he shall surely be put to death: the people of the land shall stone him with stones.*

Deut 22:24 *Then ye shall bring them both out unto the gate of that city, and ye shall stone them with stones that they die; the damsel, because she cried not, being in the city; and the man, because he hath humbled his neighbor's wife: so thou shalt put away evil from among you.*

2. The law did permit the public display or "hanging" of a lawbreaker's body "on a tree" strictly commanding that the "body shall not remain overnight on the tree but was to be buried that day." Such a practice seems to set Israel apart from other nations.

Deut 21:22 *And if a man have committed a sin worthy of death, and he be to be put to death, and thou hang him on a tree:*

Deut 21:23 *His body shall not remain all night upon the tree, but thou shalt in any wise bury him that day; (for he that is hanged is accursed of God;) that thy land be not defiled, which the Lord thy God giveth thee for an inheritance.*

THE CURSE OF BEING HUNG

1.   Those displayed or "hung" after execution by stoning for breaking Israel's law were said to be "accursed of God."

Deut 21:22 *And if a man have committed a sin worthy of death, and he be to be put to death, and thou hang him on a tree:*

Deut 21:23 *His body shall not remain all night upon the tree, but thou shalt in any wise bury him that day; (for he that is hanged is accursed of God;) that thy land be not defiled, which the Lord thy God giveth thee for an inheritance.*

Ezra 6:11 *Also I have made a decree, that whosoever shall alter this word, let timber be pulled down from his house, and being set up, let him be hanged thereon; and let his house be made a dunghill for this.*

2.   This helps explain the reference to Jesus being killed "by hanging on a tree" and the statement in Galatians that Jesus was "cursed."

Gal 3:13 *Christ hath redeemed us from the curse of the law, being made a curse for us: for it is written, cursed is everyone that hangeth on a tree:*

Acts 5:30 *The God of our fathers raised up Jesus, whom ye slew and hanged on a tree.*

Acts 10:39 *And we are witnesses of all things which he did both in the land of the Jews, and in Jerusalem; whom they slew and hanged on a tree:*

THE DEATH OF A PRINCE

1.   Jeremiah's mention of princes being "hung up by their hands" by the Babylonians. It wasn't clear whether they were tied or nailed.

Lam 5:12 *Princes are hanged up by their hand; the faces of elders were not honored.*

2.   As the son of God and a prince of the kingdom of heaven Jesus also suffered the death of princes and hung by his hands.

THE KING OF THE JEWS

The Latin cross was shaped like a lower case "t" on which it seems likely that Jesus died because it allowed room for a sign to be placed over his head indicating his crime. The sign said, "This is Jesus the King of the Jews."

Matt 27:37 *And set over his head his accusation written, THIS IS JESUS THE KING OF THE JEWS.*

AUTHORIZATION TO CRUCIFY JESUS

1. To the Jewish people, crucifixion represented the most disgusting form of death: *He who is hanged is accursed of God* (Deut 21:23). Yet the Jewish Sanhedrin sought and obtained Roman authorization to have Jesus crucified.

Deut 21:33 *His body shall not remain all night upon the tree, but thou shalt in any wise bury him that day; (for he that is hanged is accursed of God;) that thy land be not defiled, which the Lord thy God giveth thee for an inheritance.*

2. The Romans obtained authorization to have Jesus crucified.

Mark 15:13-15 *And they cried out again, Crucify him. [14] Then Pilate said unto them, Why, what evil hath he done? And they cried out the more exceedingly, Crucify him. [15] And so Pilate, willing to content the people, released Barabbas unto the, and delivered Jesus, when he had scourged him, to be crucified.*

3. At a crucifixion the victim usually was nailed or tied to a wooden stake and left to die. Crucifixion means attaching the victim with nails through the wrists or with leather thongs to a crossbeam attached to a stake. Sometimes blocks or pins were put on the stake to give the victim some support as he hung suspended from the crossbeam.

At times the feet were also nailed to the vertical stake. As the victim hung by the arms, the blood could no longer circulate to the vital organs. Only by supporting himself on the seat or pin could the victim gain relief.

4. As was the custom, the charge against Jesus was attached to the cross. He was offered a draught to deaden his senses, but he refused so there was no need for the soldiers to break his legs to hasten death.

Mark 15:33 *And they gave him to drink wine mingled with myrrh; but he received it not.*

John 19:22-23 *Then came the soldiers and brake the legs of the first, and of the other which was crucified with him. [33] But when they came to Jesus, and saw that he was dead already, they brake not his legs.*

5. John talked about the bodies not remaining on the cross because of the Sabbath day.

John 19:31 *The Jews therefore, because it was the preparation, that the bodies should not remain upon the cross on the Sabbath day, (for that Sabbath day was an high day,) besought Pilate that their legs might be broken, and that they might be taken away.*

JESUS DIED AND WAS PLACED IN A TOMB

1.   By the ninth hours, probably about 3:00 p.m. Jesus was already dead. It had only taken six hours.

Mark 15;34 *And at the ninth hour Jesus cried with a loud voice, saying, Eloi, Eloi, lama sabachthani? Which is, being interpreted, My God, my God, why hast thou forsake me?*

Mark 15:37 *And Jesus cried with a loud voice, and gave up the ghost.*

2.   Jesus' body was not left to rot; the disciples were able to secure Pilate's permission to give Him a proper burial.

John 19: 31 *The Jews therefore, because it was the preparation, that the bodies should not remain upon the cross on the Sabbath day, (for that Sabbath day was an high day,) besought Pilate that their legs might be broken, and that they might be taken away.*

SIGNIFICANCE OF THE CROSS

1.   The authors of the gospels tell us that the Lord Jesus spoke of the cross before His death as a symbol of the necessity of full commitment even unto death for himself those who would be his disciples.

Matt 10:38 *And he that taketh not his cross, and followeth after me, is not worthy of me.*

Mark 10:21 *Then Jesus beholding him loved him, and said unto him, one thing thou lackest: go thy way, sell whatsoever thou hast, and give to the poor, and thou shalt have treasure in heaven: and come, take up the cross and follow me.*

Luke 14:27 *And whosoever doth not bear his cross, and come after me, cannot be my disciple.*

2.   The willingness to suffer for our sins so that we might be reconciled to God and know his peace. Thus the cross symbolizes the glory of the Christian gospel; as a result of this humiliating and shameful death.

Phil 2:8 *And being found in fashion as a man, he humbled himself, and became obedient unto death, even the death of the cross.*

Heb 12:2 *Looking unto Jesus the author and finisher of our faith; who for the joy that was set before him endured the cross, despising the shame, and is set down at the right hand of the throne of God.*

2 Cor 5:19 *To wit, that God was in Christ, reconciling the world unto himself, not imputing their trespasses unto them; and hath committed unto us the word of reconciliation.*

Col 1:20 *And, having made peace through the blood of his cross, by him to reconcile all things unto himself; by him, I say, whether they be things in earth, or things in heaven.*

Eph 2:16 *And that he might reconcile both unto God in one body by the cross, having slain the enmity thereby:*

1 Cor1:17 *For Christ sent me not to baptize, but to preach the gospel: not with wisdom of words, lest the cross of Christ should be made of none effect.*

3.   The major significance of the cross after Jesus' death and resurrection is its use as a symbol of Jesus.

4.   The debt of sin against us was "nailed to the cross" and we have "been crucified with Christ, having been made free from sin and death made alive to God."

Romans 6:6 *Knowing this, that our old man is crucified with him, that the body of sin might be destroyed, that henceforth we should not serve sin.*

Romans 6:7 *For he that is dead is freed from sin.*

Romans 6:8 *Now if we be dead with Christ, we believe that we shall also live with him*:

Romans 6:10 *For in that he died, he died unto sin once: but in that he liveth, he liveth unto God.*

Romans 6:11 *Likewise reckon ye also yourselves to be dead indeed unto sin, but alive unto God through Jesus Christ our Lord.*

5.   The cross then is the symbol of Jesus' love, God's power to save, and the thankful believer's unreserved commitment to Christian discipleship. To those who know the salvation which Christ gained for us through his death it is a "wondrous cross" indeed.

THE CROSS A STUMBLING BLOCK FOR THE JEWS

The cross has been a major stumbling block in the way of the Jews, preventing the majority of them from accepting Jesus as the Messiah. The apostle Paul summed up the importance of the crucifixion best: *We preach Christ crucified, unto the Jews a stumbling block and to the Greeks foolishness; but to those who are called, both Jews and Greeks, Christ the power of God and the wisdom of God* (1 Cor 1:23-24).

Gal 5:11 *And I, brethren, if I yet preach circumcision, why do I yet suffer persecution? Then is the offence of the cross ceased.*

Out of the ugliness and agony of crucifixion God accomplished the greatest good of all the redemption of sinners.

CROWNS ARE SYMBOLS OF HONOR AND AUTHORITY

Crowns are worn as symbols of honor and authority.

1.   Several different words in the original Hebrew and Greek languages of the Bible are translated as crown. The high priest and the king in the early history of the nation of Israel also wore crowns as a mark of the office and authority.

Lev 8:9 *And he put the mitre upon his head; also upon the mitre, even upon his forefront, did he put the golden plate, the holy crown; as the Lord commanded Moses.*

2 Sam 1:10 *So I stood upon him, and slew him, because I was sure that he could not live after that he was fallen: and I took the crown that was upon his head, and the bracelet that was on his arm, and have brought them hither unto my lord.*

2.   Other people in the Bible are described as wearing crowns.

Esth 2:17 *And the king loved Esther above all the women, and she obtained grace and favor in his sight more than all the virgins; so that he set the royal crown upon her head, and made her queen instead of Vashti [concubine].*

3.   Crowns were also symbols of honor and authority in the Greek and Roman worlds. Jesus' crown of thorns was meant to make him an object of mockery. The Crown of Thorns was a symbol of authority fashioned by the Roman soldiers and placed on Jesus' head shortly before His death by crucifixion. They shouted, "Hail, King of the Jews," while they engaged in their cruel and brutal sport of slapping, spitting, and scourging Jesus. But Jesus' love was so strong that he endured this mockery to accomplish his mission on earth.

Matt 27:29 *And when they had plated a crown of thorns, they put it upon his head, and a reed in his right hand: and they bowed the knee before him, and mocked him, saying, Hail, King of the Jews!*

Mark 15:17 *And they clothed him with purple, and platted a crown of thorns, and put it about his head.*

Mark 15:18 *And began to salute him, Hail, King of the Jews!*

John 19:2 *And the soldiers platted a crown of thorns, and put it on his head, and they put on him a purple robe.*

John 19:5 *Then came Jesus forth, wearing the crown of thorns, and put it on his head, and they put on him a purple robe.*

John 19:15 *Then came Jesus forth, wearing the crown of thorns, and the purple robe. And Pilate saith unto them, Behold the man!*

4.   Apostle Paul wrote that men strive to obtain power and earthly kingdoms but such are temporary and corrupt. Paul sought the glory of Christ and the crown of the heavenly kingdom which was perfect and not corruptible.

1 Cor 9:25 And every man that striveth for the mastery is temperate in all things. Now they do it to obtain a corruptible crown; but we are incorruptible.

2 Tim 4:8 Henceforth there is laid up for me a crown of righteousness, which the Lord, the righteous judge, shall give me at that day: and not to me only, but unto all them also that love his appearing.

5.   The book of Revelation portrays Christ as wearing many crowns on his head, signifying his kingly authority.

Rev 19:12 *His eyes were as a flame of fire, and on his head were many crown; and he had a name written, that no man knew, but he himself.*

6.   As a reward for our faithfulness, we will receive an imperishable crown. The one that will not wither or fade away.

1 Cor 9:25 *And every man that striveth for the master is temperate in all things. Now they do it to obtain a corruptible crown; but we are incorruptible.*

James 1:12 *Blessed is the man that endureth temptation; for when he is tried, he shall receive the crown of life, which the Lord hath promised to them that love him.*

CHAPTER 20

SALVATION

In the Old Testament, salvation means deliverance from the power of sin; the word sometimes refers to deliverance from danger.

Jer 15:20 *And I will make thee unto this people a fenced brazen wall: and they shall fight against thee, but they shall not prevail against thee: for I am with thee to save thee and to deliver thee, saith the Lord.*

DELIVERANCE

1. Deliverance of the weak from oppressors.

Ps 35:9-10 *And my soul shall be joyful in the Lord: it shall rejoice in his salvation. [10] All my bones shall say, Lord, who is like unto thee, which deliverest the poor from him that is too strong for him, yea, the poor and the needy from him that spoileth him?*

2. The healing of sickness.

Isaiah 38:20 *The Lord was ready to save me: therefore we will sing my songs to the stringed instruments all the days of our life in the house of the Lord.*

3. Deliverance from blood guilt and its consequences.

Ps 51:14 *Deliver me from blood guiltiness, O God, thou God of my salvation: and my tongue shall sing aloud of thy righteousness.*

4. Deliverance also could refer to national deliverance from military threat.

Exodus 14:13 *And Moses said unto the people, Fear ye not, stand still, and see the salvation of the Lord, which he will shew to you today: for the Egyptians whom ye have seen today, ye shall see them again no more forever.*

5. Deliverance or salvation could be from captivity.

Ps 14:7 *Oh that the salvation of Israel were come out of Zion when the Lord bringeth back the captivity of his people, Jacob shall rejoice, and Israel shall be glad.*

6.   Salvation finds its deepest meaning in the spiritual realm of life. Man's universal need for salvation is one of the clearest teachings of the Bible. The need for salvation goes back to man's removal from the Garden of Eden.

Gen 3:6 *And when the woman saw that the tree was good for food, and that it was pleasant to the eyes, and a tree to be desired to make one wise, she took of the fruit thereof, and did eat, and gave also unto her husband with her; and he did eat.*

Gen 3:23 *Therefore the Lord God sent him forth from the Garden of Eden, to till the ground from whence he was taken.*

SALVATION OF NOAH

1.   After the fall, Man's life was marked by strife and difficulty. Corruption and violence dominated his world.

Gen 6:11-13 *The earth also was corrupt before God, and the earth was filled with violence. [12] And God looked upon the earth, and, behold, it was corrupt; for all flesh had corrupted his way upon the earth. [13] And God said unto Noah, the end of all flesh is come before me; for the earth is filled with violence through them; and, behold, I will destroy them with the earth.*

2.   When God destroyed the world with the flood, He also performed the first act of salvation by saving Noah and his family. These eight people became the basis of another chance for mankind.

3.   The salvation of Noah and his family was viewed by the apostle Peter as a pattern of that full salvation which we receive in Christ.

1 Pet 3:18-22 *For Christ also hath once suffered for sins, the just for the unjust, that he might bring us to God, being put to death in the flesh, but quickened by the Spirit: [19] By which also he went and preached unto the spirits in prison; [20] Which sometimes were disobedient, when once the longsuffering of God waited in the days of Noah, while the ark was a preparing, wherein few, that is, eight souls were saved by water. [21] The like figure whereunto even baptism doth also now save us (not the putting away of the filth of the flesh, but the answer of a good conscience toward God, by the resurrection of Jesus Christ: [22] Who is gone into heaven, and is on the right hand of God; angels and authorities and powers being made subject unto him.*

SALVATION OF THE EXODUS

1.   The central theme of the Old Testament experience of salvation is seen in Exodus.

Exodus 12:40 *Now the sojourning of the children of Israel, who dwelt in Egypt, was four hundred and thirty years.*

Exodus 14:31 *And Israel saw that great work which the Lord did upon the Egyptians: and the people feared the Lord, and believed the Lord, and his servant Moses.*

2.   Much of Israel's worship of God was a renewal of this mighty experience that brought them from tyranny in Egypt to freedom.

Exodus 13:3 *And Moses said unto the people, Remember this day, in which ye came out from Egypt, out of the house of bondage; for by strength of hand the Lord brought you out from this place: there shall no leavened bread be eaten.*

Exodus 13:9 *And it shall be for a sign unto thee upon thine hand, and for a memorial between thine eyes, that the Lord's law may be in thy mouth: for with a strong hand hath the Lord brought thee out of Egypt.*

3.   The Israelites formed a holy nation of priestly servants of the Lord.

Exodus 19:4-6 *Ye have seen what I did unto the Egyptians, and how I bare you on eagles' wings, and brought you unto myself. [5] Now therefore, if ye will obey my voice indeed, and keep my covenant, then ye shall be a peculiar treasure unto me above all people: for all the earth is mine: [6] And ye shall be unto me a kingdom of priests, and an holy nation. These are the words which thou shalt speak unto the children of Israel.*

GOD'S PATTERN OF SALVATION

1.   The Exodus became a pattern of salvation by which God's future deeds of redemption would be understood. But just as the Exodus symbolized their salvation, the captivity of the Israelites in Babylon was a disastrous return to bondage. The people responded to this plight with expectations of a new and better Exodus.

Is 43:14-16 *Thus saith the Lord, your redeemer, the Holy One of Israel; for your sake I have sent to Babylon, and have brought down all their nobles, and the Chaldeans, whose cry is in the ships.*

Is 43:15 *I am the Lord, your Holy One, the creator of Israel, your King.*

Is 43:16 *Thus saith the Lord, which maketh a way in the sea, and a path in the mighty waters.*

2.   God would forgive their sins and restore their hearts to faithfulness.

Jer 31:31 *Behold, the days come, saith the Lord, that I will make a new covenant with the house of Israel, and with the house of Judah:*

Jer 31:32 *Not according to the covenant that I made with their fathers in the day that I took them by the hand to bring them out of the land of Egypt; which my covenant they brake, although I was an husband unto them, saith the Lord:*

Jer 31:33 *But this shall be the covenant that I will make with the house of Israel; After those days, saith the Lord, I will put my law in their inward parts, and write it in their hearts; and will be their God, and they shall be my people.*

Jer 31:34 *And they shall teach no more every man his neighbour, and every man his brother, saying, Know the Lord: for they shall all know me, from the least of them unto the greatest of them, saith the Lord: for I will forgive their iniquity, and I will remember their sin no more.*

3.   This hope for a new Exodus merged with expectation of a full realization of the rule of God.

Ezek 36:22 *Therefore say unto the house of Israel, Thus saith the Lord God; I do not this for your sakes, O house of Israel, but for mine holy name's sake, which ye have profaned among the heathen, whither ye went.*

Ezek 36:33 *And I will sanctify my great name, which was profaned among the heathen, which ye have profaned in the midst of them; and the heathen shall know that I am the Lord, saith the Lord God, when I shall be sanctified in you before their eyes.*

Ezek 36:24 *For I will take you from among the heathen, and gather you out of all countries, and will bring you into your own land.*

Ezek 36:25 *Then will I sprinkle clean water upon you, and ye shall be clean: from all your filthiness, and from all your idols, will I cleanse you.*

Ezek 36:26 *A new heart also will I give you, and a new spirit will I put within you: and I will take away the stony heart out of your flesh, and I will give you an heart of flesh.*

Ezek 36:27 *And I will put my spirit within you, and cause you to walk in my statutes, and ye shall keep my judgments, and do them.*

Ezek 36:28 *And ye shall dwell in the land that I gave to your father; and ye shall be my people, and I will be your God.*

4.   A new understanding arose: The realization of God's purpose of salvation the coming of a completely new age.

Isaiah 65:17 *For, behold, I create new heavens and a new earth; and the former shall not be remembered, now come into mind.*

Isaiah 65:18 *But be ye glad and rejoice forever in that which I create; for, behold, I create Jerusalem a rejoicing, and her people a joy.*

Isaiah 65:19 *And I will rejoice in Jerusalem, and joy in my people: and the voice of weeping shall be no more hard in her, nor the voice of crying.*

5. References to the coming of a completely new age.

Isaiah 65:20 *There shall be no more thence an infant of days, nor an old man that hath not filled his days: for the child shall die an hundred years old; but the sinner being an hundred years old shall be accursed.*

Isaiah 65:21 *And they shall build houses, and inhabit them; and they shall plant vineyards, and eat the fruit of them.*

Isaiah 65:22 *They shall not build, and another inhabit; they shall not plant, and another eat: for as the days of a tree are the days of my people, and mine elect shall long enjoy the work of their hands.*

Isaiah 65:23 *They shall not labour in vain, nor bring forth for trouble; for they are the seed of the blessed of the Lord, and their offspring with them.*

Isaiah 65:24 *And it shall come to pass, that before they call, I will answer; and while they are yet speaking, I will hear.*

Isaiah 65:25 *The wolf and the lamb shall feed together, and the lion shall eat straw like the bullock: and dust shall be the serpent's meat. They shall not hurt nor destroy in all my holy mountain, saith the Lord.*

CHRIST'S MISSION OF SALVATION

1. During Christ's earthly ministry, salvation was brought to us.

Matt 1:21 *And she shall bring forth a son, and thou salt call his name JESUS: for he shall save his people from their sins.*

John 12:47 *And if any man hear my words, and believe not, I judge him not: for I came not to judge the world, but to save the world.*

Romans 5:9 *Much more than, being now justified by his blood, we shall be saved from wrath through him.*

Luke 19:9 *And Jesus said unto him, 'This day is salvation come to this house, forsomuch as he also is a son of Abraham.'*

2.   The salvation that comes through Christ may be described in three tenses: past, present, and future. When a person believes in Christ, he is saved, yet, just believing in Christ isn't enough. You must believe in a way of repentance.

Act 16:31 *And they said, Believe on the Lord Jesus Christ, and thou shalt be saved, and thy house.*

SAVED FROM THE POWER OF SIN

1.   We shall be saved from the very presence of sin.

Romans 8:13 *For if you live after the flesh, ye shall die: but if ye through the Spirit do mortify the deeds of the body, ye shall live.*

Phil 2:12 *Wheretofore, my beloved, as ye have always obeyed, not as in my presence only, but now much more in my absence, work out your own salvation with fear and trembling.*

Romans 13:111 *And that, knowing the time, that now it is high time to awake out of sleep: for now is our salvation nearer than when we believed.*

Titus 2:12 *Teaching us that, denying ungodliness and worldly lusts, we should live soberly, righteously, and godly, in this present world;*

Titus 2:13 *Looking for that blessed hope, and the glorious appearing of the great God and our Savior Jesus Christ.*

2.   God has released into our lives today the power of Christ's resurrection.

Romans 6:4 *Therefore we are buried with him by baptism into death: that like as Christ was raised up from the dead by the glory of the Father, even so we also should walk in newness of life.*

3.   The foretaste of our future allows us to be God's children.

2 Cor 1:22 *Who hath also sealed us, and given the earnest of the Spirit in our hearts.*

Eph 1:14 *Which is the earnest of our inheritance until the redemption of the purchased possession, unto the praise of his glory.*

4.   Our experience of salvation will be complete when Christ returns.

Heb 9:28 *So Christ was once offered to bear the sins of many; and unto them that look for him shall he appear the second time without sin unto salvation.*

5.   The kingdom of God will be fully revealed.

Matt 13:41 *The Son of man shall send forth his angels, and they shall gather out of his kingdom all things that offend, and them which do iniquity;*

Matt 13:42 *And shall cast them into a furnace of fire: there shall be wailing and gnashing of teeth.*

Matt 13:43 *Then shall the righteous shine forth as the sun in the kingdom of their Father. Who hath ears to hear, let him hear.*

CHAPTER 21

ATONEMENT

Atonement is the act by which God restores a relationship of harmony and unity between himself and human beings.

INTRODUCTION

The act by which God restores a relationship of harmony and unity between Himself and human beings. The word can be broken into three parts which express this great truth in simple but profound terms: "At-one-ment." Through God's atoning grace and forgiveness, we are reinstated to a relationship of at-one-ment with God in spite of our sin.

Because of Adam's sin and our own personal sins, no person is worthy of the relationship with a Holy God. Since we are helpless to correct this situation and can do nothing to hide our sin from God, we all stand condemned by sin.

It is human nature our willfulness and God's nature which is a Holy nature and His wrath against sin which make us "enemies." God's gift is Atonement. God's gracious response to the helplessness of His chosen people, the nation of Israel, was to give them a means of reconciliation through the Old Testament covenant law.

This came in the sacrificial system where the death and blood of the animal were accepted by God as a substitute for the death which the sinner deserved: *"For the life of the flesh is in the blood, and I have given it to you upon the altar to make atonement for your souls."*

The Law required that the sacrificial victims must be free from defect, and buying them always involved some cost to the sinner. An animals' death did not make people right with God in some simple way.

The hostility between God and man because of sin is a personal matter. God for His part personally gave the means of atonement in the sacrificial system; man and women for their part personally are expected to recognize the seriousness of their sin.

They must also identify themselves personally with the victim that dies: *"Then he shall put his hand on the head of the burnt offering, and it will be accepted on his behalf to make atonement for him."*

Although the Old Testament believers were truly forgiven and received genuine atonement through animal sacrifice, the New Testament clearly states that during the Old Testament period God's justice was not served: "For it is not possible that the blood of bulls and goats could take away sins." Atonement was possible "because in His forbearance God had passed over the sins that were previously committed."

God's justice was served in the death of Jesus Christ as a substitute who "not with the blood of goats and calves, but with His own blood He entered the Most Holy Place once for all, having obtained eternal redemption."

"And for this reason He is the Mediator of the new covenant" for our response. The Lord Jesus came according toGod's will "to give His life a ransom for many" or for all. "Through God laid on Him the iniquity of us all."

Yet Christ "has loved us and given Himself for us, an offering and a sacrifice to God" so that those who believe in Him might receive atonement and "be saved from God's wrath" through "the precious blood of Christ."

No believer who truly understands the awesome holiness of God's wrath and the terrible hopelessness that comes from personal sin can fail to be overwhelmed by the deep love of Jesus for each of us, and the wonder of God's gracious gift of eternal atonement through Christ. Through Jesus, God will present us "faultless before the presence of His glory with exceeding joy."

1.   BECAUSE OF ADAM'S SIN WE ARE ALL SINNERS

Romans 5:18 *Therefore as by the offence of one judgment came upon all men to condemnation; even so by the righteousness of one the free gift came upon all men unto justification of life.*

1 Cor 15:22 *For as in Adam all die, even so in Christ shall all be made alive.*

Col 1:21 *And you, that were sometime alienated and enemies in your mind by wicked works, yet now hath he reconciled.*

2. No person is worthy of relationship with a holy God.

Eccles 7:20 *For there is not a just man upon earth, that doeth good, and sinneth not.*

Romans 3:23 For all have sinned, and come short of the glory of God.

3. We can do nothing to hide our sin from God.

Heb 4:13 *Neither is there any creature that is not manifest in his sight: but all things are naked and opened unto the eyes of him with whom we have to do.*

4. We all stand condemned by sin.

Romans 3:19 *Now we know that what things soever the law saith, saith to them who are under the law: that every mouth may be stopped, and all the world may become guilty before God.*

5. It is human nature or our sinfulness and God's nature holy wrath against sin which makes us enemies.

Romans 5:10 *For if, when we were enemies, we were reconciled to God by the death of his Son, much more, being reconciled, we shall be saved by his life.*

6. The sacrificial system where the death, or blood of the animal was accepted by God as a substitute.

Ezek 18:20 *The soul that sinneth, it shall die. The son shall not bear the iniquity of the father, neither shall the father bear the iniquity of the son: the righteousness of the righteous shall be upon him, and the wickedness of the wicked shall be upon him.*

7. The life of the flesh is in the blood for our soul.

Lev 17:11 *For the life of the flesh is in the blood: and I have given it to you upon the altar to make an atonement for your souls: for it is the blood that maketh an atonement for the soul.*

8. For personal sin we are expected to recognize the seriousness of our sin.

Lev 16:29 *And this shall be a statute forever unto you: that in the seventh month, on the tenth day of the month, ye shall afflict your souls, and do no work at all, whether it be one of your own country, or a stranger that sojourneth among you:*

Lev 16:30 *For on that day shall the priest make an atonement for you, to cleanse you, that ye may be clean from all your sins before the Lord.*

Micah 6:6 *Wherewith shall I come before the Lord, and bow myself before the high God? Shall I come before him with burnt offerings, with calves of a year old?*

Micah 6:7 *Will the Lord be pleased with thousands of rams, or with ten thousands of rivers of oil? Shall I give my first born for my transgression, the fruit of my body for the sin of my soul?*

Micah 6:8 *He hath shewed thee, O man, what is good; and what doth the Lord require of thee, but to do justly, and to love mercy, and to walk humbly with thy God?*

BLOOD AND BURNT OFFERING

1. Laying hand on the head of the burnt offering.

Lev 1:4 *And he shall put his hand upon the head of the burnt offering; and it shall be accepted for him to make atonement for him.*

2. Blood of bulls and goats could not take away the sins.

Heb 10:4 *For it is not possible that the blood of bulls and of goats should take away sins.*

JESUS GAVE HIMSELF AS THE BLOOD SACRIFICE

Heb 9:12 *Neither by the blood of goats and calves, but by his own blood he entered in once into the holy place, having obtained eternal redemption for us.*

1. Jesus Christ came according to God's will.

Acts 2:23 *Him, being delivered by the determinate counsel and foreknowledge of God, ye have taken, and by wicked hands have crucified and slain:*

1 Pet 1:20 *Who verily was foreordained before the foundation of the world, but was manifest in these last times for you.*

3. Jesus gave his life in ransom for all.

Mark 10:45 *For even the Son of man came not to be ministered unto, but to minister, and to give his life a ransom for many.*

1 Tim 2:6 *Who gave himself a ransom for all, to be testified in due time.*

4. God laid on Jesus the iniquity of all.

Isaiah 53:6 *All we like sheep have gone astray; we have turned every one to his own way; and the LORD hath laid on him the iniquity of us all.*

2 Cor 5:21 *For he hath made him to be sin for us, who knew no sin; that we might be made the righteousness of God in him.*

Gal 3:13 *Christ hath redeemed us from the curse of the law, being made a curse for us: for it is written, Cursed is every one that hangeth on a tree:*

5. Jesus gave himself as the offering and sacrifed to God.

Eph 5:2 *And walk in love, as Christ also hath loved us, and hath given himself for us an offering and a sacrifice to God for a sweet smelling savour.*

6.   Through the sacrifice we are saved from the wrath of God.

Romans 3:22 *Even the righteousness of God which is by faith of Jesus Christ unto all and upon all them that believe: for there is no difference:*

Romans 5:9 *Much more then, being now justified by his blood, we shall be saved from wrath through him.*

1 Pet 1:19 *But with the precious blood of Christ, as of a lamb without blemish and without spot:*

CHAPTER 22

JUSTIFICATION

Justification is the process by which sinful man is made acceptable to a holy God.

Justification by Grace

Christianity is unique because of its teaching of justification by grace.

Justification is God's declaration that the demands of His Law have been fulfilled in the righteousness of His Son Jesus. The basis for this justification is the death of Christ.

The Bible teaches us that *"God was in Christ reconciling the world to Himself, not imputing their trespasses to them"* (2 Cor 5:19). This reconciliation covers all sin: *"For by one offering He has perfected forever those who are being sanctified"* (Heb 10:14).

Justification, then, is based on the work of Christ, accomplished through His blood and brought to His people through His resurrection.

When God justifies, He changes the sin of man to Christ and credits the righteousness of Christ to the believer. *"Through one man's righteous act, the free gift came to all men, resulting in justification of life"* (Rom 5:18).

Because of this righteousness "the righteousness of God" which is apart from the Law, it is through, a believer is justified from all things." God is "just" because His holy standard of perfect righteousness has been fulfilled in Christ, and He is the justifier, because this righteousness is freely given to the believer.

Justification by Faith

Although the Lord Jesus has paid the price for our justification, it is through our faith that He is received and His righteousness is experienced and enjoyed.

Faith is considered righteousness, not as the work of man, but as the gift and the work of God.

The New Testament sometimes speaks of justification as "works." For example, James spoke of justification and condemnation "by your works." The Bible said, "the doers of the law will be justified."

James concluded that *"a man is justified by works, and not by faith only."* The New Testament seems to conflict with Paul's many warnings that *"by the deeds of the law no flesh will be justified in His sight,"* and that the attempt to be justified through the law is being "estranged from Christ" and "fallen from grace."

The solution to this problem lies in the distinction between the works of the flesh and the fruit of the spirit. Not only is Christ's righteousness legally accounted to the believer, but Christ also dwells in the believer through the Holy Spirit, creating works of faith.

Certainly God's works may be declared righteous. If this is true, then the order of events in justification is grace, faith, and works; or in other words, by grace, through faith, resulting in works.

The Results of Justification

The negative result of justification is what we are saved from: *"Having now been justified, we shall be saved from wrath."* The postive result is that we are saved. "Whom He justified, these He also glorified."

The Bible also tells us "peace with God" and access to God's grace are positive benefits. The believer in Christ may look forward to the redemption of His body and eternal inheritance.

JUSTIFIED BY GRACE

1. Justification is God's declaration that the demands of his law have been fulfilled in the righteousness of his son.

Romans 3:24 *Being justified freely by his grace through the redemption that is in Christ Jesus.*

2. God was in Christ reconciling the world to himself, not imputing their trespasses to them.

2 Cor 5:19 *To wit, that God was in Christ, reconciling the world unto himself, not imputing their trespasses unto them; and hath committed unto us the word of reconciliation.*

3. This reconciliation covers all sin, for by one offering he has perfected forever those who are being sanctified.

Heb 10:14 *For by one offering he hath perfected forever them that are sanctified.*

4. Justification then is based on the work of Christ accomplished through his blood.

Romans 5:9 *Much more then, being now justified by his blood, we shall be saved from wrath through him.*

5. Christ brought to his people deliverence through his resurrection resurrection deliverance.

Romans 4:25 *Who was delivered for our offences, and was raised again for our justification.*

6. When God justifies he changes the sin of man to Christ and credits the righteousness of Christ to Him.

2 Cor 5:21 *For he hath made him to be sin for us, who knew no sin; that we might be made the righteousness of God in him.*

6. Through man's righteous act, the free gift came to all men, resulting in justification of life.

Romans 5:18 *Therefore as by the offence of one judgment came upon all men to condemnation; even so by the righteousness of one the free gift came upon all men unto justification of life.*

7. Righteousness in the righteousness of God which is apart from the law.

Romans 3:21 *But now the righteousness of God without the law is manifested, being witnessed by the law and the prophets.*

8. It is through a believer it is justified from all things.

Acts 13:39 And by him all that believe are justified from all things, from which ye could not be justified by the law of Moses.

9. Righteousness has been fulfilled in Christ and he is the justifier because this righteousness is freely given.

Romans 3:26 *To declare, I say, at this time his righteousness: that he might be just, and the justifier of him which believeth in Jesus.*

Romans 5:16 *And not as it was by one that sinned, so is the gift: for the judgment was by one to condemnation, but the free gift is of many offences unto justification.*

JUSTIFICATION BY FAITH

1. Jesus paid the price for our justification. It is through our faith that he is received and his righteousness is experienced and enjoyed.

Romans 3:25 *Whom God hath set forth to be a propitiation through faith in his blood, to declare his righteousness for the remission of sins that are past, through the forbearance of God;*

Romans 3:26 *To declare, I say, at this time his righteousness: that he might be just, and the justifier of him which believeth in Jesus.*

Romans 3:27 *Where is boasting then? It is excluded. By what law? Of works? Nay: but by the law of faith.*

Romans 3:28 *Therefore we conclude that a man is justified by faith without the deeds of the law.*

Romans 3:29 *Is he the God of the Jews only? Is he not also of the Gentiles? Yes, of the Gentiles also:*

Romans 3:30 *Seeing it is one God, which shall justify the circumcision by faith, and uncircumcision through faith.*

2. According to the Bible, faith is considered righteousness.

Romans 4:3 *For what saith the scripture? Abraham believed God, and it was counted unto him for righteousness.*

Romans 4:9 *Cometh this blessedness then upon the circumcision only, or upon the uncircumcision also? For we say that faith was reckoned to Abraham for righteousness.*

3. Righteousness is not as the works of man.

Romans 4:5 *But to him that worketh not, but believeth on him that justifieth the ungodly, his faith is counted for righteousness.*

4. Righteousness is the gift and work of God.

John 6:28 *Then said they unto him, What shall we do, that we might work the works of God?*

John 6:29 *Jesus answered and said unto them, 'This is the work of God, that ye believe on him whom he hath sent.'*

Phil 1:29 *For unto you it is given in the behalf of Christ, not only to believe on him, but also to suffer for his sake;*

JUSTIFICATION BY WORKS

1. The New Testament speaks of justification by works. Jesus spoke of justification and condemnation by your works.

Matt 12:37 *For by thy words thou shalt be justified, and by thy words thou shalt be condemned.*

2. Paul said the doers of the law will be justified.

Romans 2:13 (For not the hearers of the law are just before God, but the doers of the law shall be justified.

3. James concluded that a man is justified by works, and not by faith only.

James 2:24 Ye see then how that by works a man is justified, and not by faith only.

4. By deed of the law no flesh is justified in his sight.

Romans 3:20 *Therefore by the deeds of the law there shall no flesh be justified in his sight; for by the law is the knowledge of sin.*

5. The attempt to be justified through the law is to be estranged from Christ and fallen from grace.

Gal 5:4 *Christ is become of no effect unto you, whosoever of you are justified by the law; ye are fallen from grace.*

6. The solution to this problem lies in the distinction between the works of the flesh and the fruit of the spirit.

Gal 5:16 *This I say then, Walk in the Spirit, and ye shall not fulfill the lust of the flesh.*

Gal 5:17 *For the flesh lusteth against the Spirit, and the spirit against the flesh; and these are contrary the one to the other: so that ye cannot do the things they ye would.*

Gal 5:18 *But if ye be led of the Spirit, ye are not under the law.*

Gal 5:19 *Now the works of the flesh are manifest, which are these: Adultery, fornication, uncleanness, lasciviousness;*

Gal 5:20 *Idolatry, witchcraft, hatred, variance, emulations, wrath, strife, seditions, heresies,*

Gal 5:21 *Envyings, murders, drunkenness, revellings, and such like: of the which I tell you before, as I have also told you in time past, that they which do such things shall not inherit the kingdom of God.*

Gal 5:22 *But the fruit of the Spirit is love, joy, peace, longsuffering, gentleness, goodness, faith,*

Gal 5:23 *Meakness, temperance; against such there is no law.*

Gal 5:24 *And they that are Christ's have crucified the flesh with the affections and lusts.*

Gal 5:25 *If we live in the Spirit, let us also walk in the Spirit.*

7. Christ dwells in the believer through the Holy Spirit.

Romans 8:10 *And if Christ be in you, the body is dead because of sin; but the Spirit is life because of righteousness.*

8.   Christ the Holy Spirits creating the works of faith.

Eph 2:10 *For we are his workmanship, created in Christ Jesus unto good works, which God hath before ordained that we should walk in them.*

9.   God's work is declared righteous.

Isaiah 26:12 *Lord, thou wilt ordain peace for us: for thou also hast wrought all our works in us.*

10. This is true, then THE ORDER OF EVENTS IN JUSTIFICATION IS GRACE, FAITH, AND WORKS. IN OTHER WORDS, BY GRACE, THROUGH FAITH, RESULTING IN WORKS.

Eph 2:8 *For by grace are ye saved through faith; and that not of yourselves: it is the gift of God:*

Eph 2:9 *Not of works, lest any man should boast.*

Eph 2:10 *For we are his workmanship, created in Christ Jesus unto good works, which God hath before ordained that we should walk in them.*

THE RESULTS OF JUSTIFICATION

1.   The negative result of justification is what we are saved from: *Having now been justified, we shall be saved from wrath.*

Romans 5:9 *Much more then, being now justified by his blood, we shall be saved from wrath through him.*

2.   The positive result is what we are saved. Whom *he justified, these he also glorified.*

Romans 8:30 *Moreover whom he did predestinate, them he also called: and whom he called, them he also justified: and whom he justified, them he also glorified.*

3.   The Bible also notes peace with God and access to God's peace.

Romans 5:1 *Therefore being justified by faith, we have peace with God through our Lord Jesus Christ:*

Romans 5:2 *By whom also we have access by faith into this grace wherein we stand, and rejoice in hope of the glory of God.*

OTHER BENEFITS OF JUSTIFICATION

1. The believer in Christ may look forward to the redemption of his body and an eternal inheritance.

Romans 8:23 *And not only they, but ourselves also, which have the first fruits of the Spirit, even we ourselves groan within ourselves, waiting for the adoption, to wit, the redemption of our body.*

Romans 8:17 *And if children, then heirs; heirs of God, and joint-heirs with Christ; if so be that we suffer with him, that we may be also glorified together.*

1 Pet 1:4 *To an inheritance incorruptible, and undefiled, and that fadeth not away, reserved in heaven for you.*

CHAPTER 23

RECONCILIATION

Justification is the process by which sinful human beings are made acceptable to a holy God. Justification by Grace made Christianity unique because of its teaching of justification by grace. Justification is God's declaration that the demands of His law have been fulfilled in the righteousness of His Son. The basis for justification is the death of Christ.

Reconciliation is the process by which God and man are brought back together again. The Bible teaches that God and man are alienated from one another because of God's holiness and man's sinfulness.

Yes, God loves the sinner, but it is impossible for Him to tolerate sin. Therefore, in the biblical reconciliation, both parties are affected. Through the sacrifice of Christ, man's sin is atoned and God's wrath is appeased. Because of it, a relationship of hostility and alienation is changed into one of peace and a fellowship

Reconciliation was taken by God while we were still sinners and enemies. Christ died for us. Reconciliation is God's own completed act—something that takes place before human actions such as confession, repentance, and restitution.

God Himself has reconciled us to Himself through Jesus Christ. Paul recorded the gospel as the word of reconciliation. And knowing the terror of the Lord, Paul pleaded, implored, and persuaded men: *Be reconciled to God.*

1. According to the Bible, reconciliation is the process by which God and man are brought back together again. The Bible teaches that God and man are alienated from one another because of God's holiness and man's sinfulness.

2. One of the historic fundamentals of the faith is the vicarious Atonement, in which Christ died as a substitute for sin. The Bible tells us that God commanded His love toward us in that while we were yet sinners Christ died for us.

3. In the Old Testament, atonement was done by offering the blood of an animal sacrificed for sin, but looking forward to that ultimate sacrifice for sin was Christ. An illustration of the

REV. J. A. JEFFERSON

ultimate sacrifice for sin in found in Genesis 22:8. There Abraham said to his son, *God will provide himself a Lamb.*

Gen 22:8 *And Abraham said, My son, God will provide himself a lamb for a burnt offering: so they went both of them together.*

GOD COMMANDS HIS LOVE TOWARD US

1. In the New Testament, Christ is described as having died in the place of the Christian. This is where God had commanded His love for us, even though it was talked about long before this.

Rom 5:8 *But God commandeth his love toward us, in that, while we were yet sinners, Christ died for us.*

2. It is impossible for God not to judge sin.

Heb 10:27 *But a certain fearful looking for of judgment and fiery indignation, which shall devour the adversaries.*

3. God didn't just command His love toward us, but also the church and of the world. Paul is asking that the Ephesians to love their wives as Christ loved the church.

Eph 5:25 *Husbands, love your wives, even as Christ also loved the church, and gave himself for it;*

JESUS SENT FOR ALL THE WORLD

1. God is not only given to us but to the world as well.

Heb 2:9 *But we see Jesus, who was made a little lower than the angels for the suffering of death, crowned with glory and honour, that he by the grace of God should taste death for every man.*

2. The concept of substitutionary death is illustrated by the offering of a ram in the place of Isaac. Abraham looked up and saw a ram caught in a thicket by his horns: Which was to take the place of Isaac as the sacrifice. It seems that Abraham was willing to offer his son as requested, God was prepared to accept a substitute that He had provided.

Gen 22:13 *And Abraham lifted up his eyes, and looked, and behold behind him a ram caught in a thicket by his horns: and Abraham went and took the ram, and offered him up for a burnt offering in the stead of his son.*

3. God has reconciled us to himself though Jesus Christ.

2 Cor 5:18 *And all things are of God, who hath reconciled us to himself by Jesus Christ, and hath given to us the ministry of reconciliation.*

4.   Because Jesus died for everyone, Christians should take the message of the gospel to every creature. The first reference is found in Geneses 3:21 the primary reference Romans 5:8 and Ephesians 1:5.

Mark 16:15 *And he said unto them, Go ye into all the world, and preach the gospel to every creature.*

Gen 3:21 *Unto Adam also and to his wife did the LORD God make coats of skins, and clothed them.*

Eph 1:5 *Having predestinated us unto the adoption of children by Jesus Christ to himself, according to the good pleasure of his will.*

RECONCILED UNTO GOD

1.   In biblical reconciliation, both parties are affected. Through the sacrifice of Christ, man's sin is atoned and God's wrath is appeased. Because of the death of Christ a relationship of hostility and alienation is changed into one of peace and fellowship.

Rom 5:10 *For if, when we were enemies, we were reconciled to God by the death of his Son, much more, being reconciled, we shall be saved by his life.*

2.   Reconciliation is God's own completed act, something that takes place before human actions such as confession, repentance, and restitution. God Himself has reconcileded us to Himself through Jesus Christ.

Col 1:21 *And you, that were sometime alienated and enemies in your mind by wicked works, yet now hath he reconciled*

2 Cor 5:18 *And all things are of God, who hath reconciled us to Himself by Jesus Christ, and hath given to us the ministry of reconciliation;*

2 Cor 5:19 *To wit, that God was in Christ, reconciling the world unto himself, not imputing their trespasses unto them; and hath committed unto us the word of reconciliation.*

CHAPTER 24

REGENERATION

Regeneration is the spiritual change brought about in a person's life by an act of God. In regeneration a person's sinful nature is changed, and he is able torespond to God in faith.

The word regeneration occurs only in the New Testament, but the concept or idea is common throughout the Bible. The literal meaning of regeneration is "born again." There is a first birth and a second birth. The first, as Jesus said to Nicodemus is "of the flesh;" the second birth is "of the Spirit."

Being born of the Spirit is essential before a person can enter the kingdom of God. Every biblical command to man to undergo a radical change of character from self-centeredness to God-centeredness is, in effect, an appeal to be born again.

This great religious experience like that of Jacob at Jabbok, Moses at the burning bush, Josiah on hearing the reading of the Law, or Isaiah in the Temple might well be regarded as "new birth." This regeneration enlightening of the mind, a change of the will, and a renewed nature, a new relationship with God.

NEW TESTAMENT REFERENCE TO REGENERATION

1. Regeneration is the spiritual change brought about in a person's life by an act of God. In regeneration a person's sinful nature is changed, and he is in enabled to respond to God in faith.

Matt 19:28 *And Jesus said unto them, 'Verily I say unto you, that ye which have followed me, in the regeneration when the Son of man shall sit in the throne of his glory, he also shall sit upon twelve thrones, judging the twelve tribes of Israel.'*

Titus 3:5 *Not by works of righteousness which we have done, but according to his mercy he saved us, by the washing of regeneration, and renewing of the Holy Ghost.*

2. The literal meaning of regeneration is "born again." There is a first birth and a second birth. Jesus explained to Nicodemus (John 3:1-12).

3.   Man must undergo a radical change of character to be born again.

Psalms 51:5 *Behold, I was shapen in iniquity; and in sin did my mother conceive me.*

Psalms 51:6 *Behold, thou desirest truth in the inward part: and in the hidden part thou shalt make me to know wisdom.*

Psalms 51:7 *Purge me with hyssop, and I shall be clean: wash me, and I shall be whiter than snow.*

Psalms 51:8 *Make me to hear joy and gladness; that the bones which thou hast broken may rejoice.*

Psalms 51:9 *Hide thy face from my sins, and blot out all mine iniquities.*

Psalms 51:10 *Create in me a clean heart, O God; and renew a right spirit within me.*

Pslams 51:11 *Cast me not away from thy presence; and take not thy holy spirit from me.*

Jer 31:33 *But this shall be the covenant that I will make with the house of Israel; After those days, saith the Lord, I will put my law in their inward parts, and write it in their hearts; and will be their God, ad they shall be my people.*

Zech 13:1 *In that day there shall be a fountain opened to the house of David and to the inhabitants of Jerusalem for sin and for uncleanness.*

4.   The need for regeneration grows out of humanity's sinfulness. It is brought about through God's work in the human heart, and the person responds to God through faith. Regeneration is an act of God through the Holy Spirit, resulting in resurrection from sin to a new life in Jesus Christ.

2 Cor 5:17 *Therefore if any man be in Christ, he is a new creature: old things are passed away; behold, all things are become new.*

CHAPTER 25

FORGIVENESS

Forgiveness is the act of excusing or pardoning another in spite of slight and errors. As a theological term, forgiveness refers to God's pardon of the sins of man.

No other religious book except the Bible teaches that God completely forgives sin. The beginning comes from Him because He is ready to forgive. He is a God of grace and pardon.

Sin deserved divine punishment because it is a violation of God's holy character, but His pardon is gracious. In order for God to forgive sin, two conditions are necessary. A life must be taken as a substitute for that of the sinner, and the sinner must come to God's sacrifice in a spirit of repentance and faith.

Forgiveness is directly linked to Christ; His sacrificial death on the cross and His resurrection. He was the morally perfect sacrifice the final and ultimate fulfillment of all Old Testament sacrifices.

Since Christ bore the Law's death penalty against sinners, those who trust in His sacrifice are freed from that penalty. By faith sinners are forgiven—"justified"—in Paul's terminology. Those who are forgiven of sin's penalty also die to its controlling power in their lives.

Christ's resurrection was more than proof of His deity or innocence; it was related in a special way to His forgiveness. Christ's resurrection was an act by which God wiped out the false charges against Him. It was God's declaration of the perfect righteousness of His son.

The second Adam, and of His acceptance of Christ's sacrifice. Because He has been acquitted and declared righteous, this is also true for those who He represents. Christ's resurrection was a necessary condition for forgiveness of man's sins.

THE ACT OF FORGIVENESS

To be forgiven is to be identified with Christ in His crucifixion and resurrection. Christ has the authority to forgive sins. Thus forgiveness is an essential part of the gospel message. Blasphemy against the Holy Spirit attributing to Satan a deed done by Jesus through the power of God's Spirit which is an unpardonable sin, not because God cannot or will not forgive such a sin but because such a hard-hearted person has put himself beyond the possibility of repentance and faith.

God's forgiveness of us demands that we forgive others, because grace brings responsibility and obligation: Jesus placed no limits on the extent to which Christians are to forgive their fellow men. A forgiving spirit shows that one is a true follower of Christ.

1. Forgiveness is an act of excusing another in spite of their shortcomings. The Bible is the only religious book that teaches that God completely forgives sin.

Psalms 51:1 *Have mercy upon me, O God, according to thy loving kindness; according unto the multitude of they tender mercies blot out my transgressions.*

Pslams 51:9 *Hide thy face from my sins, and blot out all mine iniquities.*

Isaiah 38:18 *For the grave cannot praise thee, death cannot celebrate thee: they that go down into the pit cannot hope for thy truth.*

Heb 10:17 *And their sins and iniquities will I remember no more.*

2. The very beginning and essence of forgiveness comes from God.

John 3:16 *For God so loved the world, that he gave his only begotten Son, that whosoever believeth in him should not perish, but have everlasting life.*

Cor 2:13 *And you, being dead in your sins and the uncircumcision of your flesh, hath he quickened together with him, having forgiven you all trespasses;*

3. God is ready to forgive.

Luke 15:20 *And he arose, and came to his father. But when he was yet a great way off, his father saw him, and had compassion, and ran, and fell on his neck, and kissed him.*

4. God is a God of grace and pardon.

Neh 9:17 *And refused to obey, neither were mindful of thy wonders that thou didst among them; but hardened their necks, and in their rebellion appointed a captain to return to their bondage: but thou art a God ready to pardon, gracious and merciful, slow to anger, and of great kindness, and forsookest them not.*

Daniel 9:9 *To the Lord our God belong mercies and forgivenesses, though we have rebelled against him;*

Psalms 130:4 *But there is forgiveness with thee, that thou mayest be feared.*

5. Sin deserves divine punishment because it is a violation of God's holy character.

Gen 2:17 *But of the tree of the knowledge of good and evil, thou shalt not eat of it: for in the day that thou eatest thereof thou shalt surely die.*

Romans 1:18 *For the wrath of God is revealed from heaven against all ungodliness and unrighteousness of men, who hold the truth in unrighteousness;*

Romans 1:32 *Who knowing the judgment of God, that they which commit such things are worthy of death, not only do the same, but have pleasure in them that do them.*

1 Pet 1:16 *Because it is written, Be ye holy; for I am holy.*

6. A life must be taken as a substitute for the sinner.

Lev 17:11 *For the life of the flesh is in the blood: and I have given it to you upon the altar to make an atonement for your souls: for it is the blood that maketh an atonement for the soul.*

Heb 9:22 *And almost all things are by the law purged with blood; and without shedding of blood is no remission.*

FORGIVENESS IS DIRECTLY LINKED TO CHRIST

1. The sinner must come to God's sacrifice in a spirit of repentance and faith.

Mark 1:4 *John did baptize in the wilderness, and preach the baptism of repentance for the remission of sins.*

Acts 10:43 *To him give all the prophets witness, that through his name whosoever believeth in him shall receive remission of sins.*

James 5:15 *And the prayer of faith shall save the sick, and the Lord shall raise him up; and if he have committed sins, they shall be forgiven him.*

2. Forgiveness is directly linked to Christ.

Acts 5:31 *Him hath God exalted with his right hand to be a Prince and a Savior, for to give repentance to Israel, and forgiveness of sins.*

Col 1:14 *In whom we have redemption through his blood, even the forgiveness of sins:*

3. Jesus' sacrificial death on the cross.

Romans 4:24 *But for us also, to whom it shall be imputed, if we believe on him that raised up Jesus our Lord from the dead;*

4. Jesus Christ's resurrection.

2 Cor 5:15 *And that he died for all, that they which live should not henceforth live unto themselves, but unto him which died for them, and rose again.*

5. Jesus was the morally perfect sacrifice.

Romans 8:3 *For what the law could not do, in that it was weak through the flesh, God sending his own Son in the likeness of sinful flesh, and for sin, condemned sin in the flesh:*

6. Jesus was the final and ultimate fulfillment of the Old Testament sacrifice.

Heb 9:10 *Which stood only in meats and drinks, and divers washings, and carnal ordinances, imposed on them until the time of reformation.*

Heb 9:11 *But Christ being come an high priest of good things to come, by a greater and more perfect tabernacle, not made with hands, that is to say, not of this building;*

7. Jesus bore the law's death penalty against sinners.

Gal 3:10 *For as many as are of the works of the law are under the curse: for it is written, cursed is every one that continueth not in all things which are written in the book of the law to do them.*

Gal 3:11 *But that no man is justified by the law in the sight of God, it is evident: for, the just shall live by faith.*

Gal 3:12 *And the law is not of faith: but, The man that doeth them shall live in them.*

Gal 3:13 *Christ hath redeemed us from the curse of the Law, being made a curse for us: for it is written, Cursed is every one that hangeth on a tree;*

BY FAITH SINNERS ARE FORGIVEN

1. By faith, sinners are forgiven.

Romans 3:28 *Therefore we conclude that a man is justified by faith without the deeds of the law.*

Gal 3:8 *And the scripture, foreseeing that God would justify the heathen through faith, preached before the gospel unto Abraham, saying, In thee shall all nations be blessed.*

Gal 3:9 *So then they which be of faith are blessed with faithful Abraham.*

2. Those who are forgiven sin's penalty also die to its controlling power in their life.

Romans 6:4 *Therefore we are buried with him by baptism into death: that like as Christ was raised up from the dead by the glory of the Father, even so we also should walk in newness of life.*

Romans 6:5 *For if we have been planted together in the likeness of his death, we shall be also in the likeness of his resurrection;*

Romans 6:6 *Knowing this, that our old man is crucified with him, that the body of sin might be destroyed, that henceforth we should not serve sin.*

3.   Christ's resurrection was a necessary condition for the forgiveness of man's sins.

1 Cor 15:12 *Now if Christ be preached that he rose from the dead, how say some among you that there is no resurrection of the dead?*

1 Cor 15:13 But if there be no resurrection of the dead, then is Christ not risen:

1 Cor 15:14 *And if Christ be not risen, then is our preaching vain, and your faith is also vain.*

1 Cor 15:15 *Yea, and we are found false witnesses of God; because we have testified of God that he raised up Christ: whom he raised not up, if so be that the dead rise not.*

4.   Christ has the authority to forgive sins.

Matt 1:21 *And she shall bring forth a son, and thou shalt call him name JESUS: for he shall save his people from their sins.*

Heb 9:11 *But Christ being come an high priest of good things to come, by a greater and more perfect tabernacle, not made with hands, that is to say, not of this building.*

Heb 10:18 *Now where remission of these is, there is no more offering for sin.*

FORGIVENESS IS AN ESSENTIAL PART OF THE GOSPEL MESSAGE

1.   Forgiveness is an essential part of the gospel message.

Acts 2:38 *Then Peter said unto them, Repent, and be baptized every one of you in the name of Jesus Christ for the remission of sins, and ye shall receive the gift of the Holy Spirit.*

Acts 5:31 *Him hath God exalted with his right hand to be a Prince and a Savior, for to give repentance to Israel, and forgiveness of sins.*

2.   God's forgiveness of us demands that we forgive others, because grace brings responsibility and obligation.

Luke 6:37 *Judge not, and ye shall not be judged: condemn not, and ye shall not be condemned: forgive, and ye shall be forgiven;*

Matt 18:22 *Jesus saith unto him, I say not unto thee, Until seen time: but until seventy times seven.*

Matt 18:35 *So likewise shall my heavenly Father do also unto you, if ye from your hearts forgive not everyone his brother their trespasses.*

Luke 17:4 *And if he trespass against thee seven times in a day, and seven times in a day turn again to thee, saying, I repent; thou shalt forgive him.*

3. A forgiving spirit shows a true follower of Christ.

Mark 11:25 *And when ye stand praying, forgive, if ye have ought against any: that your father also which is in heaven may forgive you your trespasses.*

CHAPTER 26

ADOPTION

Adoption is the act of taking voluntarily a child of other parents as one's child; in a theological sense, the act of God's grace by which sinful people are brought into His redeemed family.

In the New Testament, the Greek word is translated as adoption literally means "placing as a son." It is a legal term that expresses the process by which a man brings another person into his family, endowing him with the status and privileges of a biological son or daughter.

OLD TESTAMENT

In the Old Testament, adoption was never common among the Israelites. Adoption in the Old Testamentwas done by foreigners or by Jews influenced by foreign customs. Pharaoh's daughter adopted Moses and another Pharaoh adopted Genubath. There doesn't seem to be another work in Hebrew to describe the process of adoption. When the Pharaoh's daughter adopted Moses, the test says, "And he became her son."

Exodus 2:10 And the child grew and she brought him unto Pharaoh's daughter, and he became her son. And she called his name Moes: and she said, Because I drew him out of the water.

NEW TESTAMENT

In the New Testament times, Roman customs exercised a great deal of influence on Jewish family life. One custom is particularly significant in relation to adoption. The Roman law required that the adopter be a male and childless; the one to be adopted had to be an independent adult, able to agree to be adopted.

THEOLOGICAL CONCEPT OF ADOPTION

In the eyes of the law, the adopted one became a new creature; he was regarded as being born again into the new family, an illustration of what happens to the believer at conversion.

The apostle Paul used this legal concept of adoption as an analogy to show the believer's relationship to God. Although similar ideas are found throughout the New Testament, the word adoption, used in a theological sense, is found in the writings of Paul.

1. In Ephesians, Paul's emphasis was that "our adoption rests with God, who predestined us to adoption as sons."

Eph 1:5 *Having predestinated us unto the adoption of children by Jesus Christ to himself, according to the good pleasure of his will.*

2. In his letter to the Romans, Paul used the term to describe Israel's place of honor in God's plan.

Romans 9:4 *Who are Israelites; to whom pertaineth the adoption, and the glory, and the covenants, and the giving of the law, and the service of God, and the promises.*

3. The believer has been given the spirit of adoption, which allows them to cry, "Abba, Father."

Gal 4:6 *And because ye are sons, God hath sent forth the Spirit of his Son into your hearts, crying, Abba, Father.*

4. The Gentile believers have also been given the "Spirit of adoption," which allows them to cry, "Abba, Father."

Romans 8:15 *For ye have not received the spirit of bondage again to fear; but ye have received the Spirit of adoption, whereby we cry, Abba, Father.*

Romans 8:23 *And not only they, but ourselves also, which have the firstfruits of the Spirit, even we ourselves groan within ourselves, waiting for the adoption, to wit, the redemption of our body.*

5. God's adoption of the believer also has a future dimension: the assurance that the believer's body will be resurrected.

Romans 8:23 And not only they, but ourselves also, which have the firstfruits of the Spirit, even we ourselves groan within ourselves, waiting for the adoption, to wit, the redemption of our body.

UNIT V:
PRAYERS

MAN'S GREAT QUESTION: ONE REQUEST AND TWO BLESSINGS

There be many that say, who will shew us any good?
Lord, lift thou up the light of thy countenance upon us.
Thou hast put gladness in my heart,
more than in the time that their corn and their wine increased.
I will both lay me down in peace, and sleep:
for thou, Lord, only makest me dwell in safety. AMEN.
(Psalm 4:6-8).

- - - - - -

I CARRY ON WITHIN MYSELF

I find that when hellos are past and friends are gone away,
I still have left that precious thing, the privilege to pray.
The right to pray is always mine, the dearest thing I own.
It can't be taken from my life like things more worldly-grown.

What joy is life! what peace of mind! How great to banish care!
And know that He will listen when I say a silent prayer.
So, make your words, you will be heard! And good will come your way,
If you will but remember its your privilege to pray.

Amen. Love Joy.

- - - - - -

A PRAYER FOR STRENGTH

Father, in the long hours of trying circumstance, when it seems that every fiber of our beings is tested, help us to understand and grant us the sufficient grace to see beyond the trials, to know and remember that at the end of every burden or sorrow there is strength, faith, wisdom, growth and peace, build in us a deeper knowledge that long suffering and endurance will grow best in the worst of times in Jesus' name. AMEN.

- - - - - -